RETURN OF THE ACTOR

RETURN OF THE ACTOR

**Social
Theory
in
Postindustrial
Society**

Alain Touraine

Foreword by Stanley Aronowitz
Translation by Myrna Godzich

University of Minnesota Press   Minneapolis

The University of Minnesota Press gratefully acknowledges
translation assistance provided for this book by
the French Ministry of Culture.

Published by the University of Minnesota Press,
2037 University Avenue Southeast, Minneapolis, MN 55414.
Published simultaneously in Canada
by Fitzhenry & Whiteside Limited, Markham.
Printed in the United States of America.
Design by Barbara Riechmann-Pederson.

Library of Congress Cataloging-in-Publication Data

Touraine, Alain.
  Return of the actor.

  Translation of: Le retour de l'acteur.
  Bibliography p.
  Includes index.
  1. Social change. 2. Social action. 3. Social
movements. I. Title.
HM101.T6513   1987   303.4   87-13558
ISBN 0-8166-1593-4
ISBN 0-8166-1594-2 (pbk.)

Contents

III. Questioning the Present

Foreword
Stanley Aronowitz

1

In the first two decades after the Second World War, social theory turned away from its classical preoccupations: the sources of social change, the place of ideology and politics in history, the character of fundamental social relations. In all of its key schools three paradigms of social structure indicated the reconciliation of social science with the prevailing social order. The "general" theorists, borrowing categories from Weber and Durkheim, sought to identify the conditions for social equilibrium.[1] Their central question derived from the remarkable survival of Western industrial capitalist societies from a prolonged period of economic crisis and war that visited physical destruction on much of Europe. They were concerned to find how societies managed to reproduce themselves. The structuralists announced the death of the subject and portrayed social processes as conjunctions and articulations of transhistorical social forms.[2] In between, theorists of the middle range confined themselves to the study of social problems arising from specific institutional contexts while implicitly following the model that social structure tends toward equilibrium.[3] The coherence of this paradigm became entirely methodological; more particularly, middle-range theory tried to emulate the quantitative procedures of the natural sciences.

In sum, social scientists turned away from the questions of historical agency, traditionally based on considerations of class and power. Exceptions were the Marxists, for whom these were the central questions, but whose fundamental dimensions were considered "given" by the presuppositions of historical materialism; and a small group of iconoclasts who, influenced by the classical traditions, including Marx, forged their own syntheses of this heritage with the new social categories that emerged out of concrete historical transformations of the twentieth century. In this tradition of heteroglossic theorizing, Alain Touraine occupies a unique position. His effort to delineate the chief features of new historical agents is matched by an unromantic but abiding interest in the fate of the working class, not only in Western Europe but at the global level. Although his major thrust is to analyze the problem of *historicity*, that is, how society, in his words, "acts upon itself" to remake social relations and, indeed, the cultural model by which we represent ourselves and act, the categories of class relations and accumulation remain crucial for his work.

Touraine is widely regarded as one of the world's major students of contemporary social movements, but in the United States, despite the publication of most of his major works in translation, his influence has until now been limited because of the dominance of other paradigms. I would like to argue that the virtual collapse of nearly all the mainstream models (the crisis in Marxism, the end of grand theorizing after Parsons, the decline and supercession of structuralism by poststructuralism) is due, in no small measure, to their inadequacy in the face of real social transformations that have undermined their presuppositions. The appearance in English of *Return of the Actor* can contribute to the revival of American social theory since it comes at a time when the question of historical agency remains one of the massive conundra of social sciences that have either denied its existence or desperately clung to older essentialist models.

The tradition of dissent in American sociology is almost fifty years old. Writing at the end of the depression, Robert Lynd, whose studies of the social structure of middle America, *Middletown* and *Middletown in Transition*, were perhaps the most influential single contribution of this discipline to America's self-understanding in the 1930s and 1940s, mounted a sharp attack on the trivialization and depoliticization of social science, which he saw as reversing the movement toward socially engaged professionalism that he had helped launch. Lynd, trained in the Chicago school of American sociology, which focused on the question of how "community" is possible in the wake of rapid urban-industrial change, nevertheless retained a wide vision of the mission of social investigation; its task was to understand the relationship between social institutions, cultural relations, and wider movements of historical transformation. Although deeply impressed by Marxist analyses of economic and class structure, he remained grounded in the traditions of American pragmatism. His *Knowledge for What?* (1939), deeply influenced by the partial merger of social science and New Deal social policy, called upon social scientists to generate knowledge that served the public interest. From this perspective the scientistic aspirations evident in the rapidly professionalized disciplines of sociology, economics, and political science amounted to nothing less than betrayal of the "progressive" ideals of the founders. Long before the seminal work of Jürgen Habermas, Lynd had insisted that the relation of knowledge and social interest was irradicably linked, and to declare otherwise was to serve conservative interests.

As the postwar celebration of American dominion in the world infected the social sciences, the tendencies that Lynd identified in 1939 were exacerbated. C. Wright Mills and Alvin Gouldner traced the surrender of social science to established power in methodological as well as political terms. In his *Sociological Imagination* (1959), Mills condemns both Parsons and Merton as theorists of the era when social theory loses its critical function and becomes a servant of power. Neither "grand theory" nor rank empiricism fulfills the classical mission of social science to link public issues with private troubles, to show that what we commonly understand as personal problems are part of large-scale social issues. Mills, always on the lookout for historical agents, investigated the class structure of United States society and discovered that only at the pinnacle of economic, political, and military power were actors to be found. Gouldner, writing in the vortex of the revival of a new radicalism which shook Western societies in the 1960s and which promised to overturn the traditional societies of the Third World, accused sociology of abdicating the responsibility of social science to explain these novel developments and, indeed, of failing to address the larger question of its own functions in a revolutionary period.[4]

Nor were dissident writers kind to the middle-range theory's antimony of grand theory, a positivism which in its American sociological incarnation presented itself not in the image of evolutionary biology, as had Parsons, but in the model of physics and chemistry. According to this paradigm, articulated best by Merton, social science cannot credibly theorize large social systems; it is better to accumulate small sucesses before generalizing to the system as a whole.[5] Social theory can become truly scientific only by spurning the temptation to speculate about matters not subject to validation. Although social phenomena do not lend themselves to laboratory experiment, that is, to action within a controlled environment, Merton insisted that investigations adopt the cultural model of the natural sciences: disinterestedness, skepticism, and open sharing of knowledge with other members of the social scientific community, that is, a commitment to collective rather than competitive relations. Further, Merton urged that social science concern itself solely with theories of the middle range—neither microscopic descriptions nor grand speculations of the type found in Parsons, Pirim Sorokin, and others who wished to jump the scientific gun. Instead, he favored a cumulative approach to the discovery of social phenomena and likened the process by which sociology might one day yield apodictic knowledge to the long march of physics and cosmology from myth to science.

For the critics, Merton's prescriptions were the mirror image of Grand Theory. Not only would social science yield the effort to understand broad historical forces, but it could no longer posit systemic conflict as a social category. Conflicts were seen by positivists as necessarily local. They were lodged typically in

existing institutions, and, while real antagonisms might be evident in these struggles for power, social theory could scarcely generalize from them because of its
methodological restrictions.

American sociology accumulated vast quantities of microstudies on such important institutions and "social problems" as crime, family relations, work, and
urban communities, and in its more microscopic variant on the character of everyday relations: personal life, ordinary interactions between individuals, power
struggles in the small group or the classroom. Even though some of these studies
were fascinating and deepened our knowledge of specific areas, history disappeared.[6] Or, to use Alain Touraine's terms, they were not comprehended as instances of the struggle of social actors over historicity, that is, over who controls
the terms of the cultural model upon which action is based.[7] Rather, the cultural
model is assumed, and social action is investigated as modes by which the
cultural model reproduces itself in social situations and is internalized by the
individual.

For the critics, sociology in the postwar period opens itself to the State. This
turn of events is not produced, at least for the most part, by design. That is,
middle-range theorizing is not *perforce* a State activity. Sociology becomes integrated with State policy precisely because the type of social knowledge produced focuses on *problems* and rarely, if ever, places these issues in a context
beyond their institutional environment. The modern State wishes to reduce social
life to a series of discrete problems subject to "treatment" through social policy.
Consequently, postwar sociology finds itself in a happy alliance with liberal elements of the U.S. State, providing background studies and in the 1950s entering
directly into the processes of policy formation. For those who perform studies for
the State, the cultural ideal of value neutrality is preserved to the extent that
policy recommendations represent deductions from empirical investigations.
On the whole, however, the close relation of the State to social science presents
few ethical issues for the latter because of the shared cultural model of liberal
evolutionism.

Lynd was unambiguously a "progressive," which in the 1930s meant affili-
ating with political forces that aimed to reconstruct the social order by redistrib-
uting power and economic resources to those most devastated by the world economic crisis. For him, as for Mills and Gouldner, social knowledge was linked to
social interest. Mills did not study the structure of American economic and political power simply because he was fascinated by the commanding heights.[8] His
political sociology was suffused with a profound search for agency, that is, for
movements and social categories capable of changing the relations of power and
domination. He was opposed, in his own colloquial phrase, to the prevailing
"setup" and studied the labor movement, white collar strata, the "cultural apparatus," managers, and knowledge producers to find elements that were both
interested in and capable of taking on history.

For the mavericks of American sociology there was no question of adopting the theoretical approach of classical Marxism, no more than of hegemonic sociology. Yet, Marx remained an important figure for them precisely because of his invocation to link social structure with history, and his insistence that social action was necessarily historical because it resulted, albeit unintentionally, in altering the existing situation. Further, Marx sought the source of historical agency within the social structure itself rather that attributing change to external forces (although the debate concerning the transition from feudalism to capitalism points to conflicting interpretations on this point). At the same time, the equally powerful vision of Max Weber influenced those sociologists searching for an alternative to the dominant paradigms. From Weber, the Americans derive their understanding of the relative autonomy of politics, and the possibility that under certain circumstances politics takes command in contemporary society. Thus the State is no longer viewed as an efflux of the relations of production or, as a forger of consensus, even less as a ''terrain'' of political contestation among divergent interest groups or classes. For Mills, the State bureaucracy must be seen as an element of the power structure with its own institutional forms, ideologies, and interests which are, in principle, not reducible to economic interests of the ruling class. Similarly, the militarization of American society is not attributed merely to problems of capital accumulation (Marxists like Paul Baran and Paul Sweezy view military spending as a form of waste production that disposes of a surfeit of economic surplus).[9] The military is an institutional order that makes alliances with the large corporations but that is not necessarily subsumed under them. Later, Gouldner is to discover, in the formation of intellectuals whose role in knowledge production becomes central to the social system, a new historical actor whose effectivity in transforming class relations cannot be ascribed merely to the capital/labor relation.

2

In the ferment of the 1960s, when in all advanced industrial countries students emerged as serious social actors, conventional sociology, as Alain Touraine in his superb study of 1968 May movement in France points out, contented itself with puerile explanations for the extraordinary militancy and strength of this outpouring.[10] Parsons greeted an audience in Berkeley, where thousands of students demonstrated for Free Speech against the repression of the ''technoversity,'' with an analysis that ascribed the causes of disruption to displaced Oedipal conflict; a former Marxist turned conservative, Lewis Feuer, relied on a degraded version of Karl Mannheim's argument concerning the problem of generations.[11] In both instances, the crucial category of historicity escaped notice; Touraine argued that, despite differences, the student movement in all advanced societies was an expression of a massive rejection of ''repression and manipulation'' by an emergent technocracy that was employing the university as a site of knowledge which had become the decisive cultural and economic category of postindustrial society, to displace the conventional actors of industrial society and their political institutions. Even as Mills had identified students almost a decade earlier as new historical agents, Touraine was able to see beyond the sterile categories of conventional social science.

His analysis of the French student movement exceeded any similar effort produced in this country. For Touraine was not content to point to the specific student grievances against the French university system, although he explored with great detail the fascinating mosaic of little groups as well as large organizations that constituted the movement. Nor was his analysis limited to the university. On the contrary, instead of theorizing in an ever narrower compass, he opened his vision outward to the crisis of Western societies. Not only did he perform a comparative study of student movements across national boundaries, but he exposed the new struggles between professionals and bureaucrats/managers that had developed in the battle over who would define the historical problematic. The same year (1969) Touraine published his *Post-Industrial Society*, subtitled in English translation *Tomorrow's Social History*, which drew more fully the wide implications of what he had observed in the May events.[12] Touraine's earlier work was concerned with labor and industrial relations as well as social movements. In the late 1950s and early 1960s, he focused on class relations and tried to discover the larger implications of changes in industrial relations.

In many ways, Touraine's work differs from that of Mills and Gouldner. For example, he explicitly disagrees with Mills's power elite image even as he holds to the existence of a "power organization" which cannot be conflated with the power of large corporations. Touraine joins in the conclusion that the State directs large sections of the economy and cannot be viewed solely as an instument of class rule. In this respect, he is among the few social scientists for whom power is not so widely diffused that to speak of classes and power organizations is meaningless. More generally, his affinity with the Americans who dissent from both pluralism and middle-range theorizing is exemplified by a consistent concern with the problem of historical agency. He may be the leading social theorist today who continues the tradition for which the problem is to discover the conditions that may produce social relations in which freedom and not repression (now covert, now overt) prevails. In short, he resumes the practice of interested, although always empirically grounded, inquiry. What marks Touraine from his sociological contemporaries is his intrepid efforts to comprehend the new without regard to possible consequences for the truth status of received wisdom.

Embedded in his specific theoretical positions is a spirit of openness. Rarely, if ever, do we find that professional commitment to conventional scientific paradigms overcomes the desire to grasp social reality. Perhaps this remarkable trait can be found in Touraine's long association with the study of social movements, which, in Henri Lefebvre's terms, frequently "belie forecasts" of the end of history, a favorite theme of social thinkers in the postwar era.[13] Touraine's study of the May movement is unmarred by myopia; he takes seriously the utopianism of student demands as historically significant actions, refusing to lapse into convenient psychologism. Similarly, whereas Daniel Bell greets the coming of postindustrial society as one more confirmation for his older thesis that contemporary democratic countries have found the mechanisms to overcome the need for ideology, Touraine understands this event as the coming to power of new social agents, which, like other historical actors, arm themselves with pathbreaking ideologies. (Gouldner's last book, *The Future of Intellectuals*, invoking somewhat different analytic categories, draws similar conclusions.)[14] And, once more swimming against the current, at a time when the social movements of the last generation have suffered significant defeats, when the old power reasserts itself in a major conservative revival in nearly all northern European countries and North America, Touraine announces the return of the actor, taking conventional social theory to task for its failure to identify his/her characteristic feature, and aiming his fire with equal force as well at new, European-based theories that have not only refused to find the social movements that struggle over historicity but declare the "death" of the subject as such. For structuralism and post-structuralism, surely the most dynamic interventions into Anglo-American social and cultural theory of the 1970s and 1980s, the concept of historical agency itself is nothing less than rank essentialism, a phrase that has become the veritable battle cry of these schools.

The term, profusely used by philosopher of science Karl Popper and emulated by Louis Althusser, Lucio Colletti of the Marxist structuralists, by post-Marxists such as Michel Foucault, Ernesto Laclau, and Chantal Mouffe, signifies the tendency of humanism of both Marxist and non-Marxist varieties to posit ultimate explanations based upon essential features of history and/or human nature.[15] Popper is quite clear about his intention: to expunge (social) science of propositions not subject to empirical test; for Althusser and Foucault, the task is to shift the object of knowledge from essences to relations.

Touraine is by no means essentialist in either his historical or epistemological perspective. For example, while retaining the centrality of class and agency to social theory, he insists that the proper knowledge object is class relations, not social class. "Social class" connotes a purely descriptive, a historical category, bereft of implied actors. In contrast, social relations implies a system of mutual determinations in which action has consequences for changing the relations of power and the shape of the system itself. Thus, class relations is both a determinate and an indeterminate category. Determinate because it specifies both a system of action and the actor that constitute it; indeterminate insofar as the struggle entails a contest over who will set the agenda of action itself, who determines the cultural model. That the student movements of the late 1960s "lost" in their quest to alter the cultural model and the power system does not, for Touraine's theory, refute the assertion that history is made rather than merely constructed by the conjunction of elements of a structured totality. For Touraine, the historical agent is not designated a priori, so the charge of reductionist interpretation cannot be laid upon him.

Unlike conventional sociology which takes "values and beliefs" as among the givens of social reality, Touraine's social theory problematizes both the cultural model upon which action occurs as well as the outcome of struggles over which model will prevail. As *May Movement* and his more recent study of the Polish Solidarity movement demonstrate, Touraine has developed a theory of social movements in terms of the leading concept of *historicity*, which may transcend the prevailing cultural model or at least puts it into question. Social movements therefore are not merely groups of actors with specific grievances within institutions; they are marked by the degree to which they act upon the prevailing cultural model. They challenge it by proposing alternatives that almost invariably appear utopian in relation to hegemonic norms and values. That Touraine speaks of the cultural model distinguishes his point of departure from that of Marxism, for which culture is derivative of the mode of production of material life. What Touraine does is to pose the mode of life, including its normative features, as the fundamental object of historical contestation. This paradigm challenges theories of blind forces—whether of the classsical Marxist or structuralist varieties—without, for a moment, denying the critical significance of struggles over accumulation, class relations, and political power as crucial elements of the social system.

While Touraine is more than a student of social movements considered as a discrete "subject matter" his theoretical head is always guided by his ethnographic sense. Social movements are not by themselves capable of transforming the cultural model, of taking control of the system of action even when they speak for wider sections of society than their own class or institutional base would suggest. Since, according to Touraine, social movements are part of the system of historical action in which they are situated, they trigger change but may not control its direction. Here Touraine clearly parts company with historicism, which posits a direct link between class struggles and the shape of social change. Class relations, modes of knowledge, forms of social organization undergo mutations in consequence of the action of society upon itself, especially the action of social movements. But, if I read Touraine correctly, the result is indeterminate from the perspective of actors precisely because it is constituted by both the action and the resistance of organizational and class relations already in existence. The interaction of organization and social movement is mediated by the mode of knowledge, the mode of accumulation, and the cultural model which "captures its creativity."

Thus, Touraine undertakes his own critique of essentialism. First, he rejects the assumption that society can be reduced to a system of values which form a set of "givens" for historical action. Second, he refuses what he calls "pragmatism," really the antinomy of the first, in which society is nothing other than interaction. Instead, in an interesting parallel to Sartre's theory of historicity, he argues that historical action must run up against the past, which, however (and in this Touraine departs from Sartre), is not merely the practico-inert (the totality of past institutionalized actions as a dead hand on the future), but a necessary aspect of the social totality.[16]

For this reason, he employs the concept, appropriated from biology, of mutation to describe social change. A mutation is always discontinuous with the past and therefore has characteristics that cannot be deduced directly from the genetic structure from which it derives. Usually mutations occur as a mechanism of adaptation to a changing enviroment. But Touraine modifies this conception by stating that we are no longer speaking chiefly of organism/environment interaction in human society, but must recognize that knowledge enables society to act upon itself, that its capacity to construct images of the way in which its relations are comprehended — in other words, it has "consciousness" — means that it also possesses historicity and that its dependence on dominating nature has become (relatively) autonomous. This is what Touraine means by postindustrial society: finally accumulating no longer exclusively frames our social existence. Thus, it is not that Marx is "wrong," but that human action has transcended the conditions that produced the paradigm (in Touraine's language, a cultural model) of economic "man." For Touraine, "work" consists not merely in interacting with nature to meet human needs, but also in work on work — self-production.

Touraine's collaborative study of the Polish Solidarity movement, published in 1983 provides a vivid example of the perspicacity of his social theory. Recall that Solidarity presents itself to Polish authorities and to itself as a trade union seeking to improve the lives of its members. But it also takes on, now directly, now covertly, the fundamental questions facing Poland and its people — the monopoly of power over the economy and over political and social life by the Communist party; the arbitrary exercise of power by the State; the widespread violations of individual and collective liberties by the constituted authorities. Touraine and his associates seek to understand Solidarity in its manifold aspects as both a social and class movement organized around its stated aims, and a struggle for a new cultural model of society as such to create itself.

"Familiarity with Solidarity should convince us — and one of the aims of this book is to help establish this belief — that men and women are not subject to historical laws and material necessity, that they produce their own history through their cultural creations and social struggles by fighting for the control of these changes which still affect their collective and in particular their national life."[17] As the authors make clear, their mode of analysis challenges two prevailing views: that every struggle against despotism in eastern Europe is doomed from

Marxist and systems associated with Durkheim and Weber, is unable to grasp. Marxism clings to the primacy of economic relations "in the last instance" or, more egregiously, lapses into a kind of technologial determinism when it asserts the primacy of the productive forces as historical category; the others have surrendered their mission to explain historical change and instead retreat to studies of the way in which microactivity reproduces the social order. For both paradigms, when the traditional forces of historicity fail, historicity yields. Social theory is reduced to critique—its ability to account for the new situation is weakened by self-doubt.

In short, the paucity of critical attention to Touraine's major works during this period of sociology's crisis may be explained by the fact that his theories, however powerful, were simply not in fashion in the 1970s, and the fashion process operates as much among intellectuals as it does in the dress industry.

Touraine's most crucial departure is that he circumvents the questions that obsess dominant theorists, particularly the effort to explain the end of the history of the idea of modernity that has marked Western societies for hundreds of years. Specifically, he does not ask how these societies maintain order in the wake of their identity crises. These explanations lead either to a celebration of serendipity, really a discourse about the impossibility of theory itself in the light of the eclipse of the conditions that gave rise to theorizing, or to the surrender of efforts to make sense of social relations, and a retreat to the situation. Of course, no student of social movements can fail to take account of the specificity of the situation. But unlike many sociologists and political scientists who are content to bring to their studies little more than an arsenal of methods and a sharp eye for the unique, Touraine retains the conviction that it is possible to make sense of history as the story of human action, that the particular may illuminate the universal or at least larger trends, and that the understanding of these may form part of the basis of a new historicity.

Touraine does not approach the social world from a distance. Rather, departing (in a double sense) from the Marxian tradition, knowledge is understood as linked to interest, in his case, the interest of emancipation. Therefore, what is important is not to explain stasis but to identify the elements that enable society to act upon itself, to overcome the historical scourge of alienation. To be sure, Touraine remains indebted to Marx insofar as he preserves the category of class as a historical agency. Classes, for Marx, struggle over the accumulation of the products of labor. Touraine amends this common understanding to include two other elements: struggles over symbolic products and beyond the prevailing socioeconomic model, struggles over historicity, that is, who will represent society to itself, not only with respect to images, but also with respect to its ethical projections for the future.

In this configuration the workers and their characteristic institution, the trade unions, do not vacate the historical stage. On the contrary, in his analysis of *Sol-*

idarity, Touraine insists that class relations are in question in this social struggle. But these relations are no longer defined in terms of the goals of Western trade unions, that is, primarily in relation to the division of economic surplus. Now, Solidarity is a social movement that speaks for those who seek to control their own historicity; its challenge to the Communist regime is a challenge to the regime's prerogatives in setting the agenda of historical action. And, for Touraine and his associates, this agenda embraces the cultural model upon which social life is constructed.

In the late 1960s, Touraine, like other theorists, announced the coming of postindustrial society. But unlike Daniel Bell, who saw in this development an extension of the end of ideology (which meant that political struggles could be reduced to problems subject to managerial solution), Touraine argues that the great social actors of industrial society no longer dominated the struggle over historicity because a new field of action had been created. "If property was the criterion of membership in the former dominant classes, the new dominant class is defined by knowledge at a certain level of education." In turn the dominated class "is defined by its dependence on the mechanisms of engineered change and hence on the instruments of social and cultural integration." Accordingly, regional consciousness and the defense of local liberties are the principal foundations of resistance to technocracy (the name Touraine assigns to the new social category that has come into existence in contemporary society which "conceives society simply as the totality of the social means needed . . . by the massive economic and political structures which direct development"). Touraine argues that the antagonisms created by the rise of management occur within knowledge communities. Knowledge has become the condition of economic and social development, but not all of those possessing "scientific and technical competence" share in the control of the large organizations set up to dispense its accumulation. These knowledge producers are alienated from the possibilities for controlling historicity by the technocracy. Since the technocracy tends to centralized power, localism and individual liberties become alternative cultural models which merge in the antitechnocratic movement within the university. So, unlike American sociologists of postindustrial society who understand the passing of the historical importance of traditional industrial classes as the dawning of a new era in which Weber's instrumental rationality finally dominates society in a way that vitiates class relations themselves, Touraine insists that technocracy is a form of ideological and cultural control over knowledge producers and acts to control historicity itself.

Return of the Actor is, first of all, a synthesis of much of his previous work. It contains all of the themes that run throughout his other books. But now two crucially new positions are articulated. First, this is his most thoroughgoing treatment of the crisis in sociology. Touraine identifies sociology with an attempt to find the basis for system integration under conditions of industrialization.

weakening of research and its subjection to the actual or supposed interests of the mighty.

Our work is located at the moment when we are probably reaching the point of the greatest breakdown of the old systems of analysis, at the same time as the current economic crisis is bottoming out. Already taking place are the transformation of cultural models and the increasingly visible emergence of a new stage of economic activity, which create an urgent need for a new reflection of the social sciences upon themselves. A century and a half ago, in the wake of the French Revolution and at the dawn of the industrial era, sociology constituted itself as a new representation of social life; shouldn't we follow the example of the classics and recognize the necessity of a renewal of social thought, comparable to the one they succeeded in carrying out?

Part I

**A
New
Representation
of
Social Life**

second, referred to as socialism, the State does not grant any autonomy to the representation of social interests.

Classical sociology was concerned with societies with a capitalist type of industrialization in which the State had little autonomy in relation to the national bourgeoisie—at least as far as the metropolitan country was concerned—and thus it hardly addressed the matter of the State, tending rather to identify the ruling class with the agents of economic development. Today, we find side by side ever more *civil* societies in which many social actors influence political decisions; we also find socialist regimes in which the State is all-powerful. It is no longer possible, then, to maintain this identity between the workings of industrial society and the movement toward industrialization. On the contrary, public opinion opposes countries that seem to no longer have a sense of the State and those in which a totalitarian State identifies itself with society.

As classical sociology built up large historical ensembles self-endowed with meaning, it reduced the analysis of social activity to an inquiry into the position of the actor in the system. A sociology of action rejects such an explanation of the actor by the system. On the contrary, it sees in all situations the result of relations among actors defined by their cultural orientations as well as by their social conflicts. If the notion of social movement figures prominently and indeed decisively in such a sociology, it is not because the social movement is an answer to a situation but rather the calling into question of the relation of domination in which an actor—let us call it the ruling class—is permitted to manage the bulk of available cultural resources. It is not enough, and even dangerous, to speak of social determinisms since the individual actor participates in the production of a situation at the same time as she or he is conditioned by it. For instance, it is true that we move about in cities that have been built up long before we came upon the scene, but it is even more true that urbanization plans convey the power relations between political and social actors.

This may serve to dispel a possible misunderstanding. Sociologists are rightly suspicious of all forms of identifications between actor and observer because the latter reduce analysis to the interpretation of a discourse and thus degrade it into what could be called a second-level ideology. A sociology of social movements, and more broadly, of social action, stands at the polar opposite of such an ideological interpretation since it distinguishes between the different significations of action and the different types of social relations in which the actor is located. On the other hand, historicist explanations that assert the historical unity of observable phenomena fall prey to the deadly disease of sociological explanation. As soon as one starts out with the notion that everything in a country refers back to its capitalist character, to its modernity, or to its national character, one steps outside the realm of evidence to enter into arbitrary interpretations. The sociology of action, and especially the method of sociological intervention that is its specific practice, are opposed to such globalism, and they seek to separate the different meanings of behavior, particularly those of conflicts, and to isolate simple elements of analysis within the complexity of historical becoming. Nothing stands further from the sociology of action than the philosophy of history. Some may tend to see in the former a new avatar of a sociology of heroism, riddled with revolutions and confrontations between the past and the future. Such a view bespeaks but blindness. It is only by speaking of the labor movement, for example, that one can free sociology from its submission to the laws of capitalism or of historical evolution, whereas those who speak of class struggle generally reduce it to the history of the contradictions inherent in capitalism. To speak of the labor movement thus runs against most current uses of this expression, in France at least, where those who invoke it in fact mean the political parties of the Left.

Today, the view of history and of progress inherited from the Enlightenment and from nineteenth-century evolutionism finds itself disqualified. But the fact that it has run out of steam should not draw attention away from social movements; on the contrary, it ought to make apparent the necessity of a type of analysis that would inquire into the production of historical situations by actors rather than put actors into history.

Wherein lies the unity of the actor, then? In what way is an actor more than a set of roles? Actors have unity and exercise regulatory and organizing control upon their activities inasmuch as they live their own historicity personally, that is, they assume the capacity to disengage themselves from the forms and norms of the reproduction of behavior and consumption, in order to participate in the production of cultural models. It is proper to human beings to ensure the hierarchy of their conducts, to valorize scientific knowledge in relation to opinion or rumor, innovation and investment in relation to routinized behavior, the good in relation to social conventions. As social life produces a higher level of historicity, actors increasingly assert the importance, and the rights, of conscience and consciousness. The history of modernity is that of a growing affirmation of conscience and consciousness against the law of the monarch, custom, interest, ignorance, or fear. Social movements, collective conducts engaged in a struggle for the management of historicity, occur only if actors are capable of rising above mere claims and even above political negotiations in order to acknowledge, and to assert, themselves as producers rather than consumers of social situations, as capable of questioning social situations rather than merely responding to them.

Social life is defined above all by the self-producing and self-transforming action that it carries out upon itself by means of investments, taking this term in a larger sense than its customary economic one, as well as by means of conflicts for the management of investments, and by the ever more acute consciousness of the actors-subjects who distance themselves from the products of their investments, recognize them as their own creations, and reflect upon their own creativity. These actors-subjects come to consider as their central value the recognition and the experience of themselves as subjects, and of others as similar to themselves only by their capacity to be subjects.

Therein lies the unity of the social system: it is the field in which historicity is produced, where social conflicts are at stake, and where the consciousness of the subject is grounded.

Crisis and Mutation

In the midst of economic expansion, such ideas seemed easier to accept; we had even thought that we could go directly, given our thrust, from an industrial society to a new type of activity and social organization. Today we live in chaos instead, and the direction and sense of transformations are far less apparent. The breakdown of old industrialization/deindustrialization is easier to perceive than the formation of a postindustrial society. The disorganization of industrial society and the crisis of the idea of society lay the ground for the emergence of a nonsocial idea of society, sometimes desperate, sometimes cynical, and sometimes in pursuit of a dream. We reject most strongly all the discourses that corresponded to the hegemony we have now lost, and to the impudent pride with which we identified ourselves for so long with the meaning of History and the realm of Reason. It is easy to understand why so many of us live in a state of crisis and reject all social thought. But such feelings cannot take the place of analysis. In any case, are they not themselves out of step as we learn to recognize the problems that confront us, as new economic instruments prove necessary, as science undergoes a transformation, and as claims of new forms of moral responsibility make themselves heard? Doesn't an image of social life that is reduced to pure change tend to favor those who are most likely to profit from such change because they are the richest, the most calculating, or the most powerful? Isn't there a danger that, under the pretext of getting rid of antiquated images of social life, one may bring back the purely political form of history that our historians have so efficiently fought against for over half a century now?

This temporary eclipse of social thought must be understood historically. First, it renders manifest the rejection of the long and dramatic hijacking of the labor movement by totalitarian power, or, at the very least, by various corporatisms and especially by the liberal character of our mode of social change. Whereas voluntarist change mobilizes values, ideas, and feelings, around the State (or around the party that seizes the State), liberal change, for its part, gives priority to transformations in the realm of culture and to the opening of markets. Only after this first phase is completed are transformed actors constituted. We are presently living a cultural mutation, a strong setting into motion of social life in which human beings, ideas, and capital circulate with greater intensity than ever before. At the same time, however, we experience the exhaustion of ancient ideas and programs. Some intellectuals may already proclaim the realities as well as the problems coming into view, but the vast number of them assume the role of preservers of obsolete ideologies, if not that of scornful critics of new ideas. Those who praise social emptiness have the merit of actively contributing to the sweeping away of the fallen leaves of ideology. Those who seek in science, and not in "ideas," an understanding of what is changing are right to prefer the practice of analysis to the interpretation of history. But the time has come to reconstruct sociology in order to understand social conduct and expectation as they actually exist. In the middle of the nineteenth century, it was necessary to dismiss the worshipers and profiteers of a sacralized and embalmed French Revolution in order to discover the realities of industrialization and of the workers' condition. This led to a more general reflection upon social life. Aren't we presently in an analogous situation? Mustn't we free ourselves from an obsolete philosophy of history in order to discover, beyond the crises and disillusions, the new actors of social life and the stakes of Europe?

I am not saying that a renewed sociology would immediately cause the extreme forms of antisociology to disappear. Such a victory is achievable only after a long series of demonstrations. And even then the right questions must be formulated before answers can be provided in this period of confusion. Let us state here some of the questions around which the existence and the reorientation of sociology depend.

The most urgent question is whether we still have a history, or whether we emerge from development in order to slide into decadence, stagnation, or regression — options that are not without advantage for a given lapse of time, and not without seduction. The second question, somewhat easier to delimit, is whether we are living through a cultural mutation or only through a set of evolutions without discontinuity with the past. This choice is well apparent in two quite different and contrasting expressions: "postindustrial society" and "third industrial revolution." It calls for studies, presently still in their infancy, of transformations in the types of knowledge, in ethical models, and in forms of production. The third question is whether new social actors have appeared. It is the most difficult of the three, since events seem to dictate a negative answer and, with it, the abandoning of the illusions of those, myself included, who have spoken of new social movements during the past fifteen years. It is not the ambition of this book to provide a definitive answer to this question, but it does aim at showing why and how the question must be asked and why it calls, I continue to hold, for an affirmative answer. When so many voices combine to repeat that there are no longer any social movements today and that it is out of sheer nostalgia for a labor movement in decline that one sets out in their search, I will state the reasons why I believe that my position is far from being condemned by historical evidence. Even the regress of the social struggles of the sixties and seventies can help us understand better the nature of the social movement that these struggles carried within themselves and to sort them out from the counterculture and the ancient ideologies with which they were intermingled.

On the global scale, the success of authoritarian States is most responsible for creating doubt about the importance of new social movements. Those who had felt solidarity for the anti-imperialist movements (such as those for the liberation of Algeria or of Vietnam) were faced, after a victory turned rapidly sour, with authoritarian, bureaucratic, ideological, and repressive instances of power. More generally, is it possible to continue to give credence to social movements when the largest and most powerful of totalitarian systems claims to derive its legitimacy from the labor movement? Nonetheless, Solidarity, in particular, has demonstrated that a totalitarian regime associated with foreign domination can repress but not eliminate social actors animated by the tenacious will to reconstitute civil society. And this demonstration is the more convincing for it applies far beyond the boundaries of Poland, where Solidarity originated; at the very same moment, a large section of Latin America in which social movements had decayed by themselves and then had been repressed by military dictatorships is returning to democracy and is witness to the reconstituting of social actors, especially labor unions.

In the West, should we really believe that the importance granted to private life is opposed to collective action? On the contrary, we could well uphold the view that private life, and more generally, the entire cultural sphere, are making their entry in the field of politics today, just as the economy did during the industrial revolution and its period. A whole set of new trends of opinion (witness the women's movement) has shown—success or failure of political organizations are not the determining criteria here—that "private life" is more than ever a public thing, the stake of a social movement, the central theme of emergent social conflicts.

The Evolution of the Social Sciences

If I speak of a "return" of the actor as opposed to his "appearance," it is because the actor has been far from absent from sociology, even if the latter could not always disengage either itself or its conception of the actor from the "progressive" philosophy of the Enlightenment or from a critique of the contradictions of capitalism. It was especially readily acknowledged that growth was easier to explain by modes of behavior than by sets of circumstances, by actions of the will rather than by material resources. May 68 was both the high point and the ruin of this viewpoint. The movement that led to the events of May, very much like the one that presently agitates German youth, set the demands of the subject against the worn-out discourses of politics, against the hypocritical quest for wealth, and against the exploitations of the Third World. During the sixties I joined the ranks of those who wrote books meant to be steps in the elaboration of an analysis of historical action. With the end of the May 68 movement, there came a long freeze during which politics, especially in France, was identified with industrialization, far from any genuine societal project. And throughout that time, intellectual life was mired under the control of a thought from which all reference to action was banished. During this era of suspiciousness, any call for a social actor was taken to be the cunning maneuver of some absolute power, be it the State, the profit motive, or anything else. And thus amid accelerating change, the idea of an immobile society imposed itself. Research was deeply affected. Teachers and social workers, convinced of their powerlessness in the face of inequalities, segregation imposed by the social order and its dominant ideology, locked themselves in a verbal radicalism that covered up very conveniently their inability to generate initiatives, if not their adoption of defensive corporatist positions. The whole of sociology disintegrated, turning into a discourse that interpreted other discourses, an ideology criticizing other ideologies, all the while remaining blind to effective behavior and situations.

The agent who was to be found in our sociology during the sixties, only to be expelled from it later, did not disappear from the social sciences, however. Historians were the ones to bring agency in, as they traveled a road that took them in the opposite direction from sociologists. During the nineteenth century, history figured at the very center of a mode of social thought that identified at once with social and economic progress and with the formation of a national State, incidentally demonstrating that the notion of society is indeed the result of a crossing between the ideas of modernization and of nation. This imperious mode of thinking weakened in the face of the rise of economism, especially at the height of the second Socialist International. Economic history, all too often limited to the study of the economic situation, and unable to link up with social history, managed to impose itself through some technical accomplishments, but at the cost of impoverishing the whole of historical thought.

Fortunately, the latter was renewed through the influence of the social sciences, which occurred in two different manners, sometimes in complementing, and sometimes opposing, each other. To limit ourselves to the French case, the dominant influence came from anthropology, perhaps because Durkheim's thought had proven itself, in the period between the two World Wars, more fertile than sociology. Hence the interest of historians such as Marc Bloch and Fernand Braudel in the study of large historical ensembles with essentially cultural rather than purely economic groundings. The influence of the structural anthropology of Claude Lévi-Strauss strengthened this tendency, especially in studies of Antiquity and of the Middle Ages. Jacques Le Goff introduced the notion of historical anthropology; Georges Duby went from the study of economic systems to that of cultural and ideological structures.

The second of these trends, although somewhat more marked by sociology, did not break with the first but rather grew out of it. Emmanuel Le Roy-Ladurie discovered, while studying the penetration of capitalism into the agrarian economy of the French province of Languedoc, that it was the permanence of rural structures rather than their economic transformation that was worthy of interest. Such a discovery was characteristic of structuralism. But, in a second phase, Le Roy-Ladurie reintroduced actors in the very midst of the structures, going from the almost static world of Montaillou to the study of the social movement that was manifest in the carnival of Romans. The study of cultures turned into a "history of mentalities," distancing itself from structuralism in order to recover the foundational inspiration of Lucien Febvre. Robert Mandrou and Philippe Aries—especially the latter—were the initiators of this evolution. It brought them close to the capital works of Michel Foucault, of a more philosophical view. Jean Delumeau, for his part, similarly realigned the study of religious feelings. The crisis of sociology prevented him, however, from coming to grips with this new history, something that did happen in the United States where the very knowledge of France came to be enriched by numerous sociohistorical studies, such as those of Charles Tilly.

Thus transformed, history was consciously able to break with the traditional historicist model and to denounce its naive naturalism, and to address the issue of the construction of the historical object, as in the case of Georges Duby with respect to the battle of Bouvines, or of François Furet in his studies of the French Revolution, always a major referent of the ideology of Progress.

Today, sociology is the laggard behind other disciplines in this vast transformation of the knowledge of social life. It urgently needs help to get out of its surly isolation and to partake of this evolution. It will be recalled that the decay of classical sociology began in the very midst of expansion. And so today, it is high time to stop confusing the sociology of crisis with the crisis of sociology, and to assess problems raised by a new type of social life, a new field of historicity, the emergence of which is less and less controvertible.

Rationale for this Book

A "return to the actor" may not be entirely obvious at the moment of my writing. This may well be an understatement: a sociology that is concerned with agency, historicity, social movements, the political representation of social claims, will certainly seem to many as being against the grain. I don't want this to be a polemical book, but I am fully aware of the fact that, as I write it, I am caught between a new disabused individualism, on the one hand, and the degenerate and bureaucratized forms of the old representations of social life, on the other. What other reason would there be for this book if not to find a way out of this double dead end of social thought in order to make a contribution to the reconstruction of sociological knowledge?

The social agent is neither the reflection of the workings (or of the "contradictions'') of society, nor the sum of individual interests and desires. As our capacity to act upon ourselves increases, notably because of science and technology, a greater number of us, as well as a larger part of ourselves, are drawn into public life. When businesses are nationalized, or even when labor rights are extended, opinion remains indifferent, but when the status of television is modified, or the rights of women are discussed (as in the debate over the advantages and disadvantages of contraception), or the problems of euthanasia, or those that arise out of genetic manipulation, are evoked, then everyone is affected and feels personally and collectively concerned. A time of emotions is once again here, in the psychological as well as in the ancient historical sense. It is a time of emotions because the new social and cultural problems that call for collective choices are present to our consciousnesses without having yet found a form of political expression. At the end of the last century, it was the labor movement that appeared to be mired on the margin of a political life cluttered with the debates of another era; today this same political life goes on endlessly debating the labor question, whereas true issues and innovations develop elsewhere.

A newer phenomenon comes into play as well. For centuries, France has handled its social problems in a protected and sheltered international setting, in which it even was dominant over certain parts of the world. Such a partial hegemony enabled it the leisure to watch over its own internal social and cultural problems without concern for matters of external threat, unlike what prevails in dominated areas, today or yesteryear. This hegemony is now gone, however. For the first time in a long, long time, Europe is not the engine behind the transformations of the world. This new state of affairs has resulted in attitudes of either abandon or of mobilizing, both of which interfere with the awareness of our own internal problems. For this reason we may be unable to give rise to social and even cultural movements that would be as pure and as autonomous as in the past. From this point of view, to speak of the return or of the disappearance of the actor is to respond to this new situation in two opposite ways: social actors are surely making a comeback but under conditions that deprive them of political and ideological expression. The antisociologists, who have followed the critical sociologists, are fascinated by the explosion of individualism and conceive of social reality as nothing but a set of constraints and external threats. According to them, nothing must stand between the individual and the State, between human rights and totalitarianism, as if there no longer were any properly social stake, as if the only struggle henceforth would pit life against death.

This situation may finally allow us to separate the problems of social life from those of historical becoming and thus to free ourselves from what still bound us to the classical models of sociology. The pre-1914 socialist labor movement spoke in the name of the future, of history and progress. Who today would have the strength and the self-assurance to speak in such a prophetic mode? Social actors no longer can speak in the name of history but only in their own names, as determinate subjects. Our epoch is no longer in the throes of scientism; it returns to moralism. We no longer demand to direct the course of things; we simply claim our freedom, the right to be ourselves without being crushed by the apparatuses of power, violence, and propaganda. The return of the actor is not undertaken in the spirit of conquest but of defense; it does not call upon individual selves to melt away in a vast collective thrust; on the contrary, it is anticollectivist and refuses to hold society, and even less the State, as its gods. It believes more in personal freedoms than in collective liberation, asserting that social life is not ordered by natural or historical laws but by the action of those who fight and negotiate in order to endow the cultural orientations they valorize with a firm social form.

In olden days, social actors protested against the traditions, conventions, forms of repression and privileges that stood in the way of their recognition. Today they protest with the same vigor, but their protest is directed against the apparatuses, discourses, and invocations of external dangers that stand in the way of the affirmation of their projects, the definition of their own objectives, and their direct engagement in the conflicts, debates, and negotiations they wish for. The return of the actor is not that of an angel but rather that of the old mole. The task of sociology is to break through the sewer of dead or perverted ideologies, as much as through the illusions of pure individualism or the fascination of decadence, in order to bring to light the presence of the actors and to help their voices to be heard. Sociologists ought then to conduct their analyses far from the discourses that a society holds about itself, and work rather in close proximity to the emotions, dreams, and wounds of all those who assume the lives of actors but are not acknowledged as such because the ideologies and the forms of political organization lag well behind truly contemporary practices, ideas, and sensibilities.

This book, which is more a stage along the way than an endpoint, more of a stimulant than a demonstration, is meant to advance a simple but demanding idea: beyond the diversity of the fields of study or of the schools, and indeed endowing it with its meaning, there obtains a unity of sociological analysis. This unity would be vainly sought in the evolutionism of classical sociology. It can be found only in a sociology of the subject. It would be a mistake to think that I argue in favor of the study of social movements in the same way that others insist on the weight of the mechanisms of social control or the complexity of instances of change; it would be even more of a mistake to think that I seek to distinguish between a "left" and a "right" sociology, that is, between ideologies. French sociologists, aware of the decay of their discipline, tend to seek the causes of this decay in quarrels between individuals, coteries of ideologies. Nothing could be further from the truth, and more dangerous, than such pseudo-explanations. The distance and the incompatibility between effectively working thoughts, no matter their divergence, is far less than that between all of them and the mass of studies without any orientation whatsoever save for an ever more artificial invocation of lifeless ideas.

I make no claims whatsoever that the principles of analysis presented here would be immediately acceptable to all, but this book is entirely free of polemical content. Even though it gives a necessarily arguable interpretation of the evolution of social thought, and especially when it treats the central notions of historicity, social movements, the consciousness of subjects, and models of development, it does so in order to better situate in relation to each other the different *areas* of sociological analysis. In speaking of social movements and of their open conflicts, one gains a better understanding of how institutions ensure their own closure as well as the order they uphold, and how relations of production are transformed into relations of reproduction. The same point of departure also sheds light on the forms of the decay of social relations and of social action, a little like the way a sociology of society was previously able to bring light to the study of what it called marginality, deviance, and anomie. Finally a sociology of change, no less than a sociology of order, must ground itself in the knowledge of systems of social relations and of their cultural stakes.

I will readily acknowledge, however, that the general framework of a sociology of action, as it is elaborated in this book, is no doubt still very much colored by my deep desire to bring out the central importance of historicity and of social movements. This *parti-pris* should only elicit however various critiques, grounded in different areas and methodological approaches, rather than wholesale rejection. The essential factor is to affirm the necessity, and the possibility, of reconstructing a sociological knowledge, capable of a coherence and a diversity that do not pale by comparison with classical sociology. The central importance that both Durkheim and Weber granted to the ideas of modernity, society, and institution did not foreshorten the distance that separated them. Why should it be otherwise when these ideas make way for those of historicity, social movement, and mode of development? Sociological thought does not demand unification in any way but it must guard itself against incoherence above all, hence the central importance of a clear definition of the debates that make for its richness and which pave the way of its progress.

These debates are of two types. First, the social field no longer encompasses the whole of experience; it is exceeded on one side by the agency specific to the State (as agent of war, peace, and historical transformation) and, on the other, by individualism, interpersonal relations, and market strategies. Where do the boundaries of the social system cut though, then, if we understand by the latter an ensemble that exerts upon itself self-organizing and regulating action? Furthermore, within the social system itself, how can we combine its two faces — the enlightened face of action and change and the shadowy face of order and crisis? An old but central problem of classical sociology emerges here, albeit in more radical guise: how to understand order and movement at the same time?

In thus seeking to formulate the great problems that agitate sociology, we soon can notice that the so-called quarrels between coteries refer back to parallel but poorly coordinated efforts to apprehend the multiple aspects of social life. The basic prerequisite for constituting a coherent knowledge of social life is that all researchers attempt, to the best of their abilities, to define their objectives, to formulate their hypotheses, and to make their arguments explicit. This is why I wrote this book.

Chapter 2
The Mutation of Sociology

The crisis of sociology has to do with its very definition. It comes from the ever-growing difficulty of maintaining the very idea of society at the center of studies on social life. It is true that we often use the word *society* in a neutral sense, so that speaking of "French society" is generally tantamount to speaking of France. But sociology originated in, and developed from, the idea that a social aggregate organizes itself around a center or around a central logic so that the diverse domains of collective life appear to fulfill institutionalized functions that are maintained by mechanisms of social control and of socialization. Such aggregates exhibit an equilibrium that does not exclude tensions or internal crises but converts the institutional mechanisms into a concrete ensemble, usually in the form of a national State. The idea of society is indeed inseparable from the predominant reality of national States, and the center or the central logic of society is almost universally taken to be the State of laws, in the English or French tradition.

This view of society actually antedates sociology and in great part was conceived in the sixteenth, seventeenth, and eighteenth centuries, that is, during the period when the idea of institution imposed itself. Locke and Montesquieu gave its classical form to this institutional image of society. It so happens that sociology comes into being when this juridical conception of social unity is called into question by evolutionism. Throughout the nineteenth century, and notably in the writings of Comte, Durkheim, Weber, and Tonnies, there develops the idea of the irresistible rise of modernity, rationalization, and secularization, destroying the old essences, bonds, and beliefs that stood in their way. The Western world, and probably all of the globe with it, thus seems locked in the historical struggle of the Enlightenment against tradition, of instrumental reason against communitarian expressivity.

Were this conception to be carried to its ultimate limit, it would destroy the very idea of society, reducing it to the generalized image of the marketplace. This modern idea of society developed, however, embodying the desire to discover order in change and to institutionalize new values. There is no doubt that this evolution favors the more central countries and social categories and therefore provokes, away from the centers of industrialization, defensive reactions that appeal to cultural particularities against the universalism of industrial and market reason. Such appeals may well nourish historical thinking but cannot bring forth new sociological conceptions since in their search for a defense against the pressures of the dominant evolutionary world, they turn to an essence and a culture and not toward forms of social and economic organization. Even industrial societies are subject to powerful romantic currents that are opposed to a modernity they consider inhuman; nonetheless social thought is essentially to be found at the point of intersection between the notions of institution and evolution. That is how sociology was constituted. Auguste Comte had to be at once a man of order and a man of progress to become the founder of sociology.

At the other extreme, Talcott Parsons, who erected the last great edifice of classical sociology, relied on an evolutionary conception powerfully rendered in the binary opposition of tradition and modernity that characterizes his analysis of action. At this high point of classical sociology, order has finally prevailed over change, and it seems possible to describe society as organized, in stable and coherent fashion, around the principles of instrumental rationality. No doubt there always remain pockets of resistance to these values as well as tensions within society, but they cannot prevent Parsons' sociology or Lipset's political philosophy from triumphing at a time when the United States is assured of its global supremacy. Society is thus the ensemble organized around a rationality that alone permits the development of calculations, exchanges, and negotiations, and which brings in addition the required answers to ceaseless situational change.

Deconstruction

Classical sociology, though always disputed by some, enjoyed majority support for a long time, as is clear from a perusal of textbooks used in the sixties and sometimes even today. Yet presently it is not only in a state of crisis but in one of unavoidable decline. Before we look at the orientation that may lead sociology out of this dead end, we need to describe more precisely the forms taken by the decay of classical sociology.

The first blows that were inflicted upon it came from within the discipline of sociology itself: from the advances in the theory of organization. The latter showed that any organization, far from exhibiting a central principle of rationality, is nothing but the unstable, weakly coherent, and constantly challenged result of social relations of all kinds, and that this is so whether under conditions of civil war or of negotiated conflict, and for all varieties of organization, both formal and informal. No other field within sociology made as decisive a contribution in the fifties and sixties. The basic principles of classical sociology were deeply affected.

Somewhat later, or in tandem, there appeared an even more radical critique of classical sociology, often called functionalism. Pushing evolutionist themes to the extreme, this critique held that social behavior could not be explained by the actors' belonging to a system but rather derives from their evolving position and their varying strategy in the face of ceaseless and multiple currents. This real abolition of the very idea of society developed in two different directions: on the one hand, toward a purely strategic view that presents actors as seeking the best and the cheapest solutions—an elitist conception since it is readily apparent that the least-favored players are forced into defensive strategies, whereas the most powerful or the richest can better spread out their risks and thus show themselves more enterprising or more innovative; on the other hand, toward a simpler presentation that conflates the actor with a consumer in search of the greatest possible satisfaction and the best buy on a set of markets—a representation of extreme individualism that pretends to be perfectly liberal but remains suspect of favoring all the manipulations that can be carried out by those who are in a position to influence demand.

In contrast to these views of the actor, there has arisen a conception of the system in which the actor no longer seems to have any grasp of the rules, of that which is no longer even the law. Some time ago, Tocqueville had shown how the breakup of bonds and of mediating bodies could lead to both social atomism and the almighty State. It is therefore natural that the crisis of functionalist sociology should have led to a growing development of critical and pessimistic analyses of social organization, with the latter being perceived then as nothing more than a system of repression, forced integration, or exclusion. It may seem strange that this type of thinking should have arisen in one of the few parts of the world where absolute States do not triumph.

General historical reasons cannot explain this happenstance. It is better understood if one considers the position of intellectuals sensitive to the disappearance of the principles that unified social experience and grounded its values, as well as to the lessening of older social struggles and of the ideologies that pertained to them. This is why it is the intellectual currents that had some ties to Marxism that have embraced these positions, in which society is conceived of less as a place of confrontation between social classes than as a space in which the logic of domination unfolds through repression mechanisms in the strict sense of the term. The most influential body of work in French social sciences in this area is cer-

altogether differently, as the result of conflictual relations between the social forces that struggle for the control of the models that govern the way in which collectivity organizes normatively its relations with the environment. I call historicity precisely the set of cultural models that rule social practices but only through social relations that are always relations of power. Such a conception does not admit of an analysis still centered on the idea of society; like organization theories, it grants the social aggregate or anyone of its subjects a very low level of stability or even coherence. It does not, however, look upon social reality as a pure system of disorderly flows. Quite the contrary, it upholds the idea of a central locus around which everything orders itself, but this locus is not constituted by a will or a power; it is a Stake: historicity as the stake in the relations and the struggles between what must still be called social classes. The relations that are established in an institutional system, or at a more limited level in organizational systems, thus appear to be governed by the state of a given field of historicity, by the relations of domination and challenge in effect between opposed classes.

This conception leads to the setting of the concept of *social movement* at the center of sociology. This term, not to be used to designate any type of force for change or for collective action, must be reserved for truly central conflicts, those that call into question the social control of historicity, of the models for the elaboration of the relations between a concrete social ensemble (which we can continue to call ''society'' for simplicity's sake) and its environment. This is a new notion in relation to everything that may have been called ''social forces,'' whether in terms of evolution (progressive forces or forces resisting progress) or of the functioning of a given system. Whether one speaks of deviance and of the tendency to rebuild the destroyed social unit, or of the internal contradictions within a system of domination, collective behavior always presents itself as a translation of mechanisms, the meaning of which remains external to the actors themselves and to their relations. It is remarkable in this context, that in our industrial societies, where the labor movement has constantly played such an important role, hardly any in-depth study has been devoted to it until quite recently. We had been content with viewing it as the latest manifestation of age-old forces propelling humankind to seek its liberation, even as merely the expansion of the contradictions inherent in capitalism, within which it was locked up and thus necessarily constrained as long as it could not escape the system of contradictions, thanks to either the knowledge of evolutionary intellectuals or an almighty State.

The idea of the social movement is thus new; it forms a recognition of the fact that actors do not limit themselves to reacting to situations but actually produce situations. They define themselves both by their cultural orientations and by the social conflicts in which they are engaged. And by cultural orientations, I do not mean values contrary to those of one's opponents, but on the contrary those held in common with them and defining the stakes of the conflict. The conflicts themselves are not zero-sum games since they aim to transform the institutional and organizational forms of collective life. Such a transformation of the field of sociology and this interpretation of the disappearance of the idea of society entail a consequence that is perhaps more important than the others. I have stated that the idea of society is inseparable from the formation and the development of Nation-States. The passage from classical sociology to a sociology of action involves the separation of that which concerns social life and that which concerns the State. As social life loses its unity, its center, and its mechanisms of institutionalization, control, and socialization, the State grows ever stronger. The realm of the One, which is no longer that of social life, turns against it. Once the One was identified with the metasocial guarantors of social order—be it God, Reason, or History. Today, however, the One is no longer metasocial, it tends to take the place of social life, to crush social relations, the multiplicity of behaviors, and the autonomy of social activities. Upon the ruins of the idea of society, there emerge and develop simultaneously, and in competition with each other, historicity, that is, societies' capacity to produce themselves, and the totalitarian States that impose principles of unity that destroy all social relations.

It would be quite wrong, then, to see in the return of the actor something like the marvelous emergence of an almost godlike human being with large possibilities of production and transformation at his or her disposal. From the same ground there springs equally, if indeed not more so, the development of a new species of States: not the despotic States of yesteryear, nor the "superactors" especially inclined to inverse their power, but indeed *totalitarian* States, that is, those whose chief function is to uproot all social life, for the greatest benefit of those who hoard power and want to rule time and space, the future, and the totality of the planet. This is the diabolical way in which the disappearance of societies has been experienced as soon as a complex society, such as Weimar Germany, found itself traversed by social movements, political processes, and organizational changes: it was swallowed up in the Nazi inferno. A similar fate befell postrevolutionary Soviet society as it was suffocated in the turn to Stalinist totalitarianism.

Hence there are two chief concrete tasks for sociology today. The first, and most important on the world scale, consists in researching and in encouraging all forms of rebirth of social life in the totalitarian States, since their labor of societal destruction is never complete or final. The other great task of sociology is to discover and to analyze, in those places where the mechanisms of functioning and social change have retained enough autonomy from State power, the new actors, the new conflicts, and especially the new stakes. This requires an often difficult break with old modes of thought, for the temptation to adapt as much as possible of yesterday's language to today's realities is always great. Just as in the nineteenth century, for quite some time, there were attempts to force the analysis of the conflicts related to industrialization, and thus to understand the labor move-ment, in the terms inherited from the French Revolution (it was the Paris Com-mune that tolled the death knell of this archaism), today we try far too often to analyze realities proper to postindustrial societies by means of notions developed for the study of industrial societies. We must especially break with the objectiv-ism to which we have become so accustomed, a principle that seemed so central to us and which consisted in relating the behavior of actors primarily to their po-sition within the social system. And yet we must effect a break with this mode of analysis, stating instead that actors' behavior must now be understood by knowl-edge of their place in the social relations through which historicity is produced. The two formulas may seem to be close, but they are not, for in the first, one separates meaning from consciousness, whereas in the second, one asserts that meaning must be grasped from an action that is itself normatively oriented, that is, through the interpretation of consciousness but without breaking from it.

Isn't it time that we resolved the crisis of sociology? Let us pay homage, to be sure, to the great works that, especially from Durkheim to Parsons, have erected classical sociology into a formidable intellectual monument, but let us do so with a view to building now a sociology called for by the problems of our times. Be-fore the rise of the "science of societies," we had the "comparative study of civ-ilization" and even the "interpretation of cultures." Today, with the waning of the historical conditions that gave forth the science of societies, we must create a sociology of action. This task is rendered more urgent by the constant threat posed to the field of social life by totalitarian forces, and by the fact that the new social movements, for their part, cannot develop as long as political actors, es-pecially the intellectuals, force them into the molds of institutional channels and languages that belong to an unrecoverable past.

Chapter 3
The Crisis of Modernity

Evolutionism

Sociology came into being as a particular way of representing social life; it is possible to trace the limits of the history of this representation, now that it is losing its explanatory power. This representation of social life was centered on the search for a solution to the problem posed by all classical sociologists and formulated most clearly by Durkheim: if modernity is change, how can a stable modern society exist? If modernization is the passage from particularism to universalism, and especially from beliefs to science, how can there continue to exist particular societies, based on particular beliefs, norms, and values?

It is easy to see that the central element in the sociological representation of social life is the idea of modernity with its evolutionist component. In this, it differs from other representations of social life; in the seventeenth and eighteenth centuries, especially, the essential problem was to understand how order can prevail over disorder, private interests, and aggressivity. What we now call sociology introduced, with Auguste Comte, the idea that modern society no longer has a specific content, that it is ''positive'' and defined by its capacity to apply the universal principles of Reason to all particular situations. It is an open and free society which, at the same time, is capable of generating a perfect and absolute order, imposed by a State power that identifies with science and with the natural laws of historical evolution. Talcott Parsons' pattern variables, which express clearly and systematically this general definition of modernity, help us understand why modern sociology, when it tries to explain the phenomena it observes,

The Separation of Society and State

It obviously follows from the preceding discussion that no state can henceforth be posited as the representative of modernity, of progress, etc; hence, inevitably, a divorce occurs between political history and sociology in the strict sense of the term, disciplines so intimately conjoined within classical sociology. A remarkable expression of this dissociation between the mode of functioning and the mode of transformation of a society is provided by the Japanese example, especially as perceived by Americans, in whose eyes it constitutes a formidable challenge. One can indeed judge American society to be far more *modern* than Japanese society, according to the generally accepted conception of modernity; yet, at the same time, one is forced to acknowledge that Japanese society is the more *modernizing* of the two: its growth level, during the long period of expansion that began after the Second World War, was four times higher than that of the United States, itself half as large as that of Western Europe, incidentally. Americans have identified themselves, and been identified by others, with the very image of modernity. This conception continues to be acceptable today but only on the explicit condition that modernity and modernization, the inseparable notions of the classical sociological model, now become separated.

Bismarck's Germany, Meiji Japan, postwar France—all have been led by elites that were simultaneously traditionalist and modernizing, and not by the most modern, market-oriented, groups. These ruling elites were far more motivated by the will to ensure national independence, to build a genuine State, or to erase a humiliation than by an ideal of rationalization. This is how Japan has managed to build a highly efficient industry while preserving and generalizing modes of social and economic organization considered traditional and even archaic by the prophets of modernity. This in no way proves that a given model of development is superior to another, but it does bring out perfectly the distinction that has established itself between the two types of problems constituted by the functioning of a given type of social organization, on the one hand, and the historical transformation of a country, on the other, or, in more concrete terms, the problems of industrial society and those of industrialization.

Political life is increasingly identified with the management of the economy; social life, with cultural behavior and personality problems. The traditional field of sociology is divided thereby. On one side, we see a resurgence of political theory, long held in check by the idea that political institutions did no more than reflect social forces and interests. On the other, social life is less and less analyzed as a system ruled by a structure and by internal laws of organization; it takes on the appearance of a network of social relations between actors oriented at least as much by their own projects and strategies as by their definition in terms of status and role.

The most visible result of this dissociation is the weakening in representation of political institutions. Even in democratic countries an ever larger gap develops between the political actors who must find a mode of representation and the political forces that are supposed to represent them. Political parties are increasingly conceived as "political businesses," whereas social claims are expressed more directly through social movements quite distinct from the parties. To define political ideas and passions is to abide by an obsolete image of political life. There are no longer any political passions, whereas the French Revolution of 1848, or the Soviet Revolution, were periods during which all passions were political.

Economic Development

In the Western industrial countries, during their period of rapid growth, the analysis of modernity was more important than the study of industrialization. Even the student rebellions attacked society from within, rather than referring to the image of a different future. Their chief objective was not to pave the way for bright tomorrows, but to live differently, and to do so right away. In the rest of the world, by contrast, problems of development, of industrialization, of national liberation have become more important than the internal problems of a societal type. Classical sociology limited itself to the study of advanced Western societies, relegating all others to anthropology. Today, sociology must study three worlds: the first, that of the advanced industrial societies of the West; the second, which corresponds to Communist countries; and the Third World.

Sociology has by no means recognized this obligation, in spite of all the interest generated by some large comparative studies (notably those of Barrington Moore, Jr. and Reinhard Bendix) or by Marxist research like that of Immanuel Wallerstein.[1] We continue calling those who study Europe or North America, sociologists, and those who study Africa, Africanists. But today the theories of modernity that place all countries on a general scale of modernization appear so blind to the differences in the forms, paths, and mechanisms of historical transformation that they are attacked as the ideological expression of the hegemony of the North over the South. Facing the materialist evolutionism of the West, the Third World is invoking more and more often an idealist and voluntarist culturalism, the intellectual and political consequences of which are as negative as those of the hegemony in the Western mode. In nineteenth-century Europe, there had already developed such an opposition between two ideologies: English or French evolutionism against German cultural historicism. Today the latter has conquered not only countries of belated capitalism like Japan, or even Brazil and Mexico, but most of the Third World, whereas Anglo-French materialism prevails in the Communist world. In the Third World, the analysis of a social system is replaced by the history of a country, itself subordinated to the idea of a national or regional essence. Internal conflicts appear to be subordinated to external conflicts between nationals and foreigners. National independence seems to be a more important goal than freedom or equality.

Today, at the end of the twentieth century, all over the world, the State — especially in its Communist or nationalist form, but the entrepreneur-State of the large capitalist countries as well — seems to occupy the entire social scene. Its domination appears so absolute that many wonder whether the era of civil societies has not come to an end and whether we are not returning to a time marked by the confrontation between empires. This is why the strongest motivation of sociologists must be to show that, behind the most powerful empires, social life has not disappeared, can reappear any-and everywhere, that it cannot be reduced to a process of historical development, and conversely, that the problems of the historical existence of a country cannot be reduced to its internal social problems, that is, that there cannot be any wholly endogenous process of historical change.

Chapter 4
Does Social Life Have a Center?

In a world dominated by war, by state nationalism, by accelerated industrialization, and within which the transmission of sociocultural inheritance looks more problematic every day as national societies grow more heterogeneous, is there still room for the idea of a stability of the social system around a central principle, whether one conceives of the latter in the form of beliefs, values, basic rights, or, on the contrary, as something that rests upon the hegemony of a dominant class or that of an omnipresent State? Must we instead invoke the Greek aphorism *panta rhei,* "everything is change"? or is it still possible to put forward a new definition of the unity of the social system?

Organization theory and decision theory are today the main forms of a sociology of change opposed to classical sociology, which was a theory of order. Their key idea is that society is centerless and that it changes only when it must adapt to alterations in the environment or resolve internal tensions. Breaking with the notion of rationality that had been used by engineers such as Taylor and Ford, this sociology speaks of limited rationality, that is, of strategy, or, as in the case of Michel Crozier,[1] of competition for the control of areas of uncertainty where the position of agents remains unclear. In this theory, social agents seek to maximize their interests, but they do so in an environment they control, or even know, only partially. The result is a series of changes played out one at a time, with no room for any principle of the unity of social life, be it central values or absolute domination.

A similar orientation is to be found in the industrial relations school, mostly American and British. For Clark Kerr or John Dunlop, just as much as for Allan

Flanders and Hugh Clegg,[2] the situation of wage earners has been altogether transformed by collective bargaining and the handling of labor claims, so that both the notion of rationalization and that of class struggle have turned into unilateral principles of explanation that express more the ideologies at stake in social conflicts than the actual processes through which these conflicts are institutionalized.

Finally, the importance given, especially in the United States, to problems of minorities, derives from the same set of analyses, even though this thinking is often associated with radical positions whereas organization theories go hand in glove with liberal or even unabashedly conservative options, and the study of collective bargaining seems to be more a middle-of-the-road pursuit.

In all three of these areas, the central belief of classical sociology in an interiorized process of modernization is questioned and ultimately rejected by virtue of the fact that no single actor can be considered the bearer of the one and only rationality: each one of these defends determinate interests and submits to group identifications in accordance with defensive as well as offensive strategies. What these various representations of social life have in common is that all structural problems seem to have been eliminated from them in favor of a single type of reality: change, or rather, changes. Those who analyze the present situation in terms of crisis and of crisis management go the farthest in destroying every central principle of social life.

The Return of the Subject

The crisis in our conception of society leads to the following conclusion: doesn't the observation of own societies show that they are progressively losing all unity, as they become richer in diversity? After a period of integrating and assimilating minorities, our countries accept an increasing degree of diversity and disintegration. This tendency seems to be greatest in Western Europe, where nations are losing their features as States since they can no longer make basic decisions about war and peace, and even important economic decisions are to a large degree no longer theirs to make. Similarly, in the rest of the world, the twentieth century has been dominated by modernizing and authoritarian States, just like the nineteenth had been by national bourgeoisies, especially by the British bourgeoisie. Communist and nationalist regimes impose the unity of their ideology and of their political objectives, so that there seems to be nothing between diversified, or even disintegrated, societies, and authoritarian empires.

The chief interest of the pragmatic conceptualization of society is that it has destroyed the illusion, born in the eighteenth century, of a natural or scientific society governed by Reason and interest. Its own image of an open, uprooted, and constantly changing society reveals, by contrast, that the evolutionist conception of society we had evoked in the beginning still subjected social life to an external principle of unity: the meaning of History. The "good society" was not a purely civil society but still represented a mixture of social integration and historical progress. It did not separate out the State, chief agent of historical transformations, from civil society as network of social relations. This is why the concept of institution has figured so prominently and so centrally in classical sociology: it belongs equally to both domains, to social life and to the State. In short, these critical analyses have shown that the classical image of society did not define the conditions of integration of a social system but rather imposed a teleological image of historical change. As a result, not even the values of modernization would figure at the center of the analysis; that place was to be occupied by the action of the State as agent of a metasocial principle, the meaning of History.

But isn't there another type of criticism that could be raised against the classical idea of society? Instead of saying that modernization abolishes every principle of the unity of social life, replacing structure by change and values by strategies, couldn't one say that the older principles of the unity of social life, which were all in some way metasocial, are being replaced slowly by a new principle of unity: the growing distance between the production and the reproduction of social life? So the unity of modern societies ought not to be defined as a passage from culture to nature, or from passion to interest, but as a movement for the liberation of human creativity.

What is new here is the fact that the unity of social life is no longer derived from the idea of society. To the contrary, what is called society is considered henceforth more as a set of rules, customs, and privileges against which individual and collective efforts at creation must always struggle. In this view, all metasocial principles of the unity of social life are replaced by the accomplishments of human labor, and, somewhat more generally, by *freedom*. The central role reserved by classical sociology for rationalization and modernization now goes to freedom and, even more profoundly to the concept of the *subject* inasmuch as it represents human beings' capacity to free themselves of both transcendental principles and community rules. The notion of subject, which still had a materialist connotation at the time of the Renaissance, has been identified from the Reformation onward with the idea of consciousness, an idea that grew in importance throughout the nineteenth century. Humankind no longer took the guise of master of Reason and Nature but as creator of the Self. This idea gave birth to one of the literary genres most typical of the West: the *Bildungsroman,* from Goethe to Styron, and going through Flaubert, Thomas Mann, Gide, and Hemingway, among others. To stress the subject and consciousness provides a modern and entirely secular principle of unity for social life, which can then be defined independently of any intervention by the State.

The decay of the idea of society thus gives birth, on the one hand, to the idea of permanent change, that is, to a wholly political conception of political life, but also, on the other hand, to the idea of the subject, whose creative capacity takes the place of the older principles of the unity of social life. The essential fact here is that the subject can no longer be defined in historical terms. Society used to be in history; now history is within societies, and they have the capacity to choose their organization, their values, and their processes of change without having to legitimate these choices by making them conform to natural or historical laws.

The critiques addressed to humanism, especially by Michel Foucault, have the merit of having contributed to the elimination of all postreligious appeals to essences, natural laws, and permanent values. But they do not bear upon the idea of the subject since the latter is the exact opposite of an essence and has no permanent substantial content.

This general transformation of sociological analysis can be expressed concretely by giving a new meaning to two traditional notions. The first is the notion of *historicity*. Until now this word has simply indicated the historical nature of social phenomenon, and its practical effect was to be found in a call for a historical type of analysis for social facts. It has seemed necessary to me to use the word in quite a different way, as I have already done in this book, to mean the set of cultural, cognitive, economic, and ethical models by means of which a collectivity sets up relations with its environment; in other words, produces what Serge Moscovici has called a "state of nature," that is, a culture. The importance given to this notion indicates that the unity of our society can no longer be found in either its internal working rules or in its place on a long evolutionary line, but indeed in its capacity to produce itself. The second notion is that of *institution,* which today must not mean that which has been instituted but that which institutes, is the mechanism through which cultural orientations are transformed into social practices. In this sence all institutions are political.

It is particularly useful to insist upon the idea of subject because of the continued pervasive power of a naturalist conception of society. But one must not separate the capacity for self-production of social actors from the distance they must maintain vis-à-vis their own works in order to acquire or keep this capacity to produce. Conversely, it is imperative to insist upon the idea of self-production at a time when the crisis in industrial values is leading quite a few thinkers to imagine a new type of society that would be concerned more with its equilibrium and its relations to the environment than with its own transformation. Actually, one could defend the idea that following a period of intense and creative criticism of industrial culture, we are today on the threshold of new forms of technical activity, which constitute a postindustrial society that is also a hyperindustrial society. So we are once again led to consider our social life as being ruled both by its creative capacity and by the situation of our nations within the totality of the world.

The Role of the Central Conflict

Historicity is not a set of values solidly established at the center of society; rather it represents a set of instruments, of cultural orientations, through which social practices are constituted, and thus one can say it is a set of investments. Investments, it needs to be recalled, are never controlled by the whole of a group. Albert Hirschman[3] was right in critiquing the recurrent populist illusion according to which the traditional society can have its best features preserved by modernization, and modernization can be accomplished without having to go through a proletarianization of the Western type or a lost generation as in the Soviet Union. Historicity, considered as a set of resources drawn from consumption, is controlled by a specific group that identifies with it and identifies it in turn with its own interests. The rest of the population, especially those upon whom rests this process of investment through the deprivation of their consumption, seek to protect themselves from the ruling group and to recover control of historicity. Thus, stressing concepts such as subject and historicity by no means leads to an idealist or moralist sociology; on the contrary, such thinking is necessarily linked to an acknowledgment of the central role of conflicts, in particular the existence of a central conflict, in modern societies.

These conflictual groups can be called *social classes*, but this term runs the risk of casting more confusion than light on the subject. Marx was referring to a fundamental contradiction between nature and society, between productive forces and the social relations of production; it seems to me that we must define classes in another way — as groups that are opposed to each other in a central conflict for the appropriation of the historicity toward which they are oriented and which constitutes the stakes of their conflict. For example, in industrial society, the conflict does not pit capitalists against proletarians (that is, workers deprived of all forms of property) but industrialists against workers. The two groups have the same cultural orientations: both believe in progress, in deferred gratification, in a repressive control of sexuality, but, at the same time they fight each other for the social control of this industrial culture in order to give different social forms to the same cultural orientations. The central social mechanism is the conflict through which a field of historicity, a set of cultural models, is transformed into a system of social relations that are always unequal relations, relations of power.

We must reject both the Parsonian idea of a society organized around a set of values specified into social norms and embodied in organizations, statutes, and roles, and the opposite idea of a social life divided into totally separate worlds corresponding to two social classes, so that anything that would seem to be common to the whole of society would be nothing but an illusion in the service of the interests of the dominant class.

Once we define the subject through creativity, and we drop the evolutionist view of society, we can bring together the idea of a central social conflict with the idea of action as oriented toward values. Cultural orientations are no longer principles, then, but cognitive, economic, and ethical investments that are transmuted into social practices through a class conflict. Industry, science, and secularization have brought forth industrial society, but they were able to do so only through the class conflict that pitted industrialists — whether private or public, native or foreign — against workers, in particular specialized craft workers who have been everywhere the originators and the backbone of unions and of socialist movements. The opposition between a definition of classes as sets of conditions and a definition of classes as actors that are both oriented toward values and engaged in a social conflict is so important that it seems preferable from my perspective, to speak of *social movements* rather than social classes, even though it is impossible to give up the term *classes* to designate the social categories referred to by organized social movements.

The three central elements of social life are therefore: the *subject,* as distanciation of organized practices and as consciousness; *historicity,* as the set of cultural models (cognitive, economic, and ethical) and as the stake of the central social conflict; and *social movements,* as the groups that contend in order to give these cultural orientations a social form. The elements can be combined in different ways. The *epic* view of social life, which lays stress on historicity, predominated under conditions of voluntary modernization, especially after the Soviet revolution. The *dramatic* view, which finds the conflict between social movements to be of greatest importance, is the most common in the Western world, where both industrialists and unions have access to political influence and to the media. Today we are tired of the historical prophecies that have led to nothing but authoritarian regimes and doctrinaire interpretations, hence the new stress on the notion of subject, which successfully conveys the distance that individuals and collectives put between themselves and institutions, practices, and ideologies. This third view of society can be called *romantic.*

There is no perfect balance point between the epic, drama, and romanticism. Indeed it is one of the functions of intellectuals to remind the social milieu in which they live that every society tends to forget or marginalize one or even two of these "climates" of social life, and it is possible that we are heading into a period when the role of social movements will be less visible, following a period when countercultural movements have reflected the role of historicity. This does not mean a shift from public problems to private business, from historicism to narcissism, but more likely that we are on the threshold of a new level of historicity; after a long period of political beliefs and a short period of purely critical thought, we are about to step into a new phase of consciousness, of a romantic affirmation of the subject, that is, into a phase necessary for reestablishing the distance between established practices and collective action, which is a precondition for new discoveries, new creations, and the formation of new social movements.

From the foregoing analyses, I conclude that the chief task of sociology is to discover—beyond customs, rules, and rituals—the cultural orientations and the contending social movements from which most social practices derive, directly or indirectly. Instead of describing the mechanisms of a social system, of its integration and disintegration, of its stability and its changes, sociologists must return to the study of social responses to analyses of mechanisms of social self-production. And since these mechanisms are neither factors nor material bases of social organization but unequal relations among actors with the same cultural orientations, our role is to explain not behavior through conditions, but, on the contrary, conditions through actions.

PART II

A
Sociology
of
Action

Chapter 5
Eight Ways of Getting Rid of the Sociology of Action

All approaches that reject the analysis of the relations between social actors are alien to sociology or even opposed to it. This is as true of approaches that reduce the meaning of action to the consciousness of the actor as of those that explain it through the latter's "circumstances." Sociology has everything to lose in pretending that it is multiple and devoid of principles adhered to by all who invoke its name. On the contrary, it must assert itself as "relational" analysis, equally removed from subjectivism and objectivism.

Within these limits, the sociology of action lies at the center of sociological analysis. It is the ground from which other territories can be explored and from which light can be shed on the other side of society, that is, the order that covers up, in the name of the power it evidences, social actions and relations. This is the only ground to be acknowledged by a sociology of action. Just as we must get rid of the opposition, alien to sociology, between objective determinants and the intentionality or the will of the subject, we must equally acknowledge that the system of relations between actors and social ordering complete and oppose each other and indeed intermix constantly. All societies can and must be analyzed as a system of social relations; all societies are politically and ideologically ordered as well. Sociology, like society, lives in perpetual tension between movement and order. The first is the locus of both cultural innovations and social conflicts, whereas the second is that of political powers and ideological categories.

The two categories should be neither separated nor confused: a sociology of movement that would ignore the constraining forces of order would give in to the illusions of a purely liberal vision and see society as a market; such a sociology

47

would be no more than the ideology of the dominant groups, which always tend to appeal to freedom of transactions inasmuch as they know they are in a position of strength. Conversely, a pure sociology of order, forgetting that order results from conflicts and transactions, would be led to derive the analysis of society from a nonsocial principle (despotism, rationality, or some combination of both); this can only feed into a political ideology to the detriment of sociology. Hence I offer the following polemical reflections, which are directed against eight approaches that contradict the principles of a sociology of agency.

Evaluating a Social Situation or Behavior
on the Basis of a Nonsocially Defined Principle

The oldest rule of sociological thought, powerfully asserted by Durkheim, is to explain the social only by the social. And yet it is difficult to implement: the sociologist may be impelled, for instance, by a moral protest. The exhaustion of workers, once it is recognized, may lead one only to denounce inhuman assembly-line labor; one can even begin to think that cities with a high density of cars do not constitute a "natural" environment for human beings. Such assertions are devoid of any sociological meaning since they stand in the way of making manifest the social relations that have produced the situations causing the indignation. This refusal to analyze social relations is very strong in the historical situations in which the most basic social conflicts, namely clan conflicts, are little organized, which is the situation that obtains when a new type of society is being set up. The ruling class tends to hide behind the "natural" evolution of things and to oppose its will to modernize to the resistance to progress. For their part, the social categories that are in the position of dominated classes erect principles and values against a management of society that they are not yet in a position to challenge head on.

Sociologists find themselves subjected today, in the industrialized countries at least, to these opposed yet combined pressures. For two decades, they have been exposed to the ideology of a new ruling class which spoke of nothing but adaptation to change, modernization, and dissolution of ideological and social confrontations. More recently they have been drawn to the utopias that have challenged this far-from-disinterested optimism, and they have proved sensitive to protests, in the name of Humankind or of Nature, against a destructive progress.

The present task of sociology, which corresponds to the rediscovery of its permanent object, is to investigate the new relations and the new social conflicts that are coming into being in a deeply transformed cultural field. We must reject equally integration, a nonsocially defined modernity, and a general critique formulated in the name of a nonsocial principle. We are getting out of a lengthy period during which sociology could only be rejected or deformed. The moment has come to give it its rightful place and to teach our society to speak sociologically. The naive belief in modernization, abundance, or scientific and technological revolution becomes untenable as political and social conflicts multiply within nations and among them.

Reducing a Social Relation to an Interaction

The object of sociology is to explain the behavior of actors through the social relations in which they find themselves. The behavior cannot be explained by the consciousness of the actors themselves, owing to the fact that there is no way of overcoming the discrepancy among the representations that actors have of their interactions. How do we choose between the worker's or the boss's image of a labor conflict? The relations and not the actors should be studied.

But nothing could be farther from this definition than reducing sociology to the study of interactions, for the latter takes the actors as its point of departure before examining their conduct toward one another. Sociology should never underestimate the study of interactions, but it must not divorce it from the recognition of the field of relations. Social actors are not sellers and buyers in a simple exchange relations reducible to a zero-sum game.

The most classical sociology has rightly shown that roles are defined by a mode of organization. The field of an interaction is defined by an intervention of society upon itself, and, as a result, all relations bring together unequal actors by the very fact that any relation, directly or indirectly, relates an actor who is directing this intervention with one who is on the receiving end of it. All social relations include power relations. There is no purely horizontal social relation.

At the simplest level, within an organization, the role of the worker and that of the shop steward are defined by an authority system that was not produced by the concerned parties but was imposed upon them either by the decision of management or as a result of collective bargaining. At a higher level, that of political institutions, actors define themselves by their influence over decisions that are recognized as legitimate. Still their position has been defined by legal rules — legislation or constitution in particular — that refer back to a social regime, that of the right of private property for example. The inequality among the actors stems from their links to the principles and the interests in which the political "rules of the game" are grounded. Finally, at the highest level, the relations between classes are not merely conflictual: classes fight for control of the cultural field, for the management of the means whereby the society "produces" itself, that is economic accumulation, a mode of cognition and a representation of the capacity that a society has to act upon itself, which I call the *ethical model*.

The opposition of classes to each other is inseparable from this action of society upon itself, of its "historicity." The superior class identifies itself with historicity and, in return, identifies it with its own interests. And the dominated class protests against this identification, fights for a collective reappropriation of the means whereby a society acts upon itself.

It is difficult to accept this conception of social relations because we are constantly influenced by our lived experiences. There, our relations are established in a "situation." Rules, norms, and social organization seem to preexist, to be given, like a theater stage with its props set out at the moment when the actors walk out on it. This view of things must be completely reversed if we are to engage in sociological analysis. If situations preceded relations, where would they come from if not from some *Deus absconditus,* some hidden God, some metasocial principle, or some natural laws—all means of placing limits on knowledge? Sociological "realism" is but an illusion. Rules do not come before acts. They are at once produced, modified, and challenged by each action. Order is neither intangible nor coherent. It is but a partial imposition of form upon social relations, cultural transformations, and conflicts of power, influence and authority. Hence the importance of social movements which bring out the most basic social relations and reveal that institutions and forms of social organization are produced by social relations instead of constituting a "state" of society that would somehow determine social relations.

Separating Systems from Actors

Every sociologist knows that the meaning of behavior cannot be conflated with the consciousness of actors. Isn't the definition of sociology as the study of systems of social relations but another way of asserting the necessary separation of systems from actors? Actually, such a separation is indispensable but in a very specific sense. A system of social relations is a construct of sociological analysis and thus does not correspond directly to any precise historical "case," whereas an actor is always a protagonist and the actions of an actor are always events; to understand them, it is necessary to mobilize a plurality of situations, that is, a plurality of social relations. It will be readily admitted that sociological analysis will not have recourse to the idea of a "human nature," to intangible values and principles, whereas actors do in fact account in this way for their own conduct, invoking the Beautiful or the Good, human rights or the civilization of the spirit of the Renaissance or German civilization.

It is not enough, however, to recall these basic principles of all sociological analysis. What is at stake here is the nature of that which explains social behavior. First, we will set aside explication by means of situations since this expression is confusing. It is difficult to see how one could explain a particular behavior by a salary level or a type of dwelling or a state of techniques. One must first transform these "situations" into social relations, and most important, into levels of participation. There does exist a new elaborate form of explanation of be-

havior through situations: couldn't a society be located along the axis of an evolution from the simple to the complex, from the undifferentiated to the
differentiated, from slow and discontinuous change to rapid and unceasing transformations, from a low to a high density of exchanges? Integration and deviance,
consensus and conflict could also be explained by organizational features or
even, in Durkheim's phrase, by social morphology. Such an evolution admits of
recognition and interpretation in quite different terms, however. What at first appears as "natural" diversification is nothing but the extension of society's action
upon itself. A complex society is, at a deeper level, a society that is much more
engaged in self-production than a less complex society, and therefore it reproduces itself less. It is thus a society in which the field of social relations and conflicts is ever growing. This means in turn that we remain within the realm of social relations just when we thought we were about to exit from it.

A view of society as the stakes of conflicts can appear only when society assumes the totality of its experience instead of limiting the field of social action to
a narrow band stuck between a metasocial order and ordering structures present
in society as well as around it. Presociological images of society are dominated
by dualistic conceptions: that which bears meaning stands above society, and the
latter is the realm of its fall, of inertia, of particular interest and arbitrariness.
Whereas conflict must stand at the center of societal analysis, presociology put
contradictions there: between practical reasons and values, meaning and nonsense, forces of production and social relations of production. As a result, a central, and properly unexplainable, role had to be assigned to actors capable of
overcoming the contradiction, bearers of meaning and eradicators of nonsense,
and representations of the universal—which nearly always turned out to be the
State.

It is not at all by chance that sociology develops at the same time as social
movements that claim the right to be the bearers of their own meaning instead of
being the servants of the party or of intellectuals or, beyond them, of the State.
Societies gain a sociological self-understanding only when they stop recognizing
the existence of a metasocial order (divine providence, principles of political order, economic laws) and are permeated by the inventions of a new culture and
generalized conflicts around the social control of this culture.

Questioning the Relative Importance
of a Given Category of Social Facts (Economy, Politics, Ideology)

It is not easy to find out why social thought was led to use such categories, and
to speak in particular of economic, political, or even more curiously "social,"
"factors." Would economic, political, or cultural facts somehow not be social?
What are the boundaries of such a reduced realm of the "social?" Actually, this

classification does no more than evidence the broad divisions of governmental action: modern states have ministers for economics, social affairs, and so on.

These commonsensical observations show the arbitrariness of the categories invoked. For example, what is generally called politics is made up of two quite distinct components: on the one hand, the representation of special interests in the making of decisions that are imposed on all the members of a territorial collectivity; on the other, the realm of the State, the power to rule, to wage war, make peace, and manage changes.

In the same way, when we speak of the economy, we sometimes mean the marshaling of material resources to accomplish some political objectives that are themselves subordinated to cultural values, and sometimes, quite to the contrary, we mean the social forms of collective work and the use of its products which are then considered as the very basis of society. Each of these terms therefore has at least two major meanings.

Given this confusion, there has been a tendency to invoke a hierarchy of needs, going from the material necessities for survival to the most "arbitrary" and most luxurious forms of culture. *Primum vivere*. This view is part of the general image of historical evolution, according to which "primitive" people would have addressed basic needs, whereas technological progress and resources would have made possible the spread of "civilization." Prudence and decency mandate that we put a stop to this type of argument, which is both ridiculous and hateful.

Annales school historians have been wiser in setting up an opposition between different temporalities. The long haul *(longue durée)* would be the time of the relations between humans and nature, whereas the short haul *(temps court)* would be that of political events. This representation embodies a simple idea: the hierarchy of temporalities and factors would go from the most "natural," the most removed from human intervention, to that which is most completely definable by means of interactions, and thus most given to change. It also corresponds to the conception that industrial society has of itself, for such a society is convinced that its material labor is essential and that political interventions and cultural "works" are determined by the state of work. But it is difficult for contemporaries of Hitler, Stalin, Mao, or even Castro, Nasser, or Boumedienne, to accept that political events are but small waves carried on the top of a deep swell of economic situations, whereas the economic and social policies of many countries appear to determine the condition of productive forces rather than be determined by it. More generally, the image of more "artificial" activities coming to crown putatively "natural" ones must be rejected, since the latter are as culturally and socially determined as are ideologies or works of art. It is up to anthropology to preserve us here from the justificatory rationalizations through which industrial societies have described their social experience.

These remarks should suffice to show that categories such as the economic, the political, or the cultural have no demarcable contour and that they do not resist even the most cursory of examination. Their *raison d'être* is to be found in a historically located ideology.

In turn, this leads to the conclusion that what we have taken to be categories of social facts are in actuality "metasocial" categories, images of a higher order that supposedly rules social facts. The weaker a society's capacity to act upon itself, the more removed the metasocial order appears to be from society, and the more endowed with the "meanings" of human behavior. Progress of historicity, of the capacity for self-production of societies, and thus the extension of the field of acknowledged social actions, have brought about advances in secularization and the weakening of metasocial guarantors of the social order. Culture, politics, economy—all opposed to society—are nothing but principal and successive, forms of the metasocial order.

In the societies that could deal with the production of consumer goods, historicity takes on the guise of a nearly identical double of human activity, but it is located transcendentally. This metasocial order can be called cultural, or more correctly, religious. Societies that deal with the distribution of goods, which we call *market* societies, conceive of the metasocial order as guarantor of exchanges, which are the motors of change. An order of rules and laws, a political order imagined and codified the principles of political law. Industrial society, for its part, can deal not only with the reproduction of consumer goods and the distribution of goods, but also with the organization of labor, and therefore it comes to believe that economic facts rule over the social order.

Since the application of science and the creation of technologies have made it possible to deal not only with consumption, distribution, and the organization of labor but also upon the ends of production and upon cultural behavior, the separation of the social from the metasocial has lost all sense. It is useless to debate the relative importance of economic and social factors since there can no longer be a boundary between these two domains. In the industrial age especially, hasn't the economy become political?

It turns out, then, that the categories of social facts are but the remains of metasocial orders invoked by past societies to give themselves a representation of both reality and the limits to their action upon themselves. Sociology cannot make any of these categories. On the contrary, it must destroy them constantly and replace them with its own labor, that is, with categories of social relations.

Putting Emphasis on Values

The most general problem of sociological analysis is to understand how a society can be one and divided at the same time. Some want to see the division only as if society were a battlefield or a market in which actors pursue individual goals of survival, of wealth, or of conquest. As Durkheim had already observed at the end of the nineteenth century, this view does not account, however, for what is often called "norms." Actually, the most important social conflicts cannot be reduced to "sharing the pie" — I deliberately use this expression to show the extent to which a purely conflictual conception of society is conservative. Revolutionary thought seeks to both destroy one order and implement another one, or to free all human beings. It certainly does not limit itself to the defense of one side, but it does legitimate the action that it defends in the name of general principles. In the same way, a ruling class assumes, or wants to assume, the totality of a society, and in particular technological or economic rationality.

Homo homini lupus is not a slogan for a protest movement. A conflict is important, or indeed it is a real social conflict, only inasmuch as the actors on both sides aim to take hold of the management of their interaction. The labor movement has not opposed to capitalism an entirely different culture and society; on the contrary, it has sought a collective reappropriation of the forces of production and of the very idea of progress. Bosses and workers have fought over and for the direction of industrialization, in its dual dimension of economic reality and cultural project.

Conversely, another strand of social thought lays stress on social unity above all. Here society is taken to be analogous to a person, in the position of the head of a family or of a corporation, who sets goals and determines the means for achieving them, regulates the relations among the members of the group, and ensures its integration and the preservation of its values. Such a sociology of social order makes *values* a key term: values are the general cultural orientations of a society, and they govern collective life through specification into social norms, which in turn are translated into forms of organization and into roles. There is no need to describe this view at length here, for it long presided over academic sociology until there were felt the deep and lasting effects of the student movement and the more general moral crisis of Western societies in response to the war in Vietnam and to the disorganization of the international monetary and economic system. This image of society is as unacceptable as the one described earlier. Even though it is true that there is no important conflict without a deeper agreement of the contending parties with respect to the stakes of the conflict, it is false to believe that the interacting actors appeal to the same norms and to the same values.

How do we get out of this double dead end? First, by dispelling a confusion and then by separating two terms abusively brought together. The confusion obviously accrues to the nature of the unity principle, which could be named simply *culture*. If by culture is meant the whole of the ideological discourses inculcated to the populace in order to ensure and legitimate order and established privileges, it is clear that it is not the stakes of social conflicts but an instrument in the service of those who hold social power. When functionalist sociology invokes values as the principle, of social integration, it is vulnerable to political criticism that rightly takes it to task for espousing the views of the rulers. One must separate carefully the unity of the historical action system that I am speaking about from these legitimating discourses of the established order. Yet such a separation is assured only if one distinguishes cultural orientations, which constitute the historical action system, from social norms, which are merely instruments for reproducing and legitimizing the established order.

What needs to be broken up is the following simple sentence: "Cultural values turn into social norms as they are applied to specific areas of social life." There is no continuity between values and norms, or more precisely, between cultural orientations and ideologies. Between values and norms are inserted, like a splitting wedge, relations of domination and thus social movements. Cultural orientations are the stakes in relations of domination; social norms evidence the hold of the ruling class over cultural orientations and are therefore challenged by the lower classes, which justify their struggle by appealing to the cultural orientations of their society. The function of the notion of the value is to cover up the gap between cultural stakes and social interests, to occult the laws of class conflicts. It is well and good for an ideological critique to unveil the role of a notion apparently alien to social conflicts, but it is not enough if this critique did not lead to the discovery, beyond the values of legitimation, of the cultural orientations absolutely linked to the historicity of a society. These orientations are to be found at the deepest level of social action—the level of productive forces, one could call it—provided it were recognized that they are not material forces but cultural action. All of society is framed between cultural orientations and values, between the instruments of societal self-production and the instruments for the reproduction of inequalities and privileges.

Considering Society as the Discourse of the Ruling Class

The ruling class would not deserve its title if it did not have the power to marshal political institutions, the State apparatus, and cultural organization in the defense of its interests and the reproduction of its privileges. Its ideology does not leave itself open for a direct confrontation with a lower-class ideology; it hides behind abstract principles or supposed technical constraints. Criticism is necessarily directed against this ideological hold and its pretenses.

But it is far from the same thing to recognize this hold and to believe that the whole of the categories of social practice represents a coherent implementation of dominant ideology. In fact such a belief is not compatible with the recognition of class relations and struggles: how can one simultaneously proclaim the unity and the integration of a social order dominated by the positivity of a power or that of an ideology, and assert that society is riddled with fundamental social conflicts? On the contrary, to assert the central importance of class relations requires that one recognize in the social organization the concrete traces of conflict, and therefore that one see equally in political institutions some capacity for action on the part of lower classes. How could one speak of the working class and of capitalist exploitation in industrial society, if the labor movement could not come into being, if workers were entirely "alienated," if unions did nothing but accept the logic of the dominant system, if the political and legal system constantly and absolutely rejected the demands and claims of organized labor and denied it any influence over labor law.

It is strange, parodoxical even, that the image of a society reduced to the reproduction of class power has been so frequently invoked in recent years in the societies in which the institutionalization of conflicts is most developed and in which these conflicts are given the broadest political, social and ideological recognition. One could understand such thinking in an autocratic, a despotic, or a totalitarian society; one would then seek to show that all categories of social practice refer back to a unified project of domination. And yet it bears repeating that such a project could not be identified with class domination since it would be viable only at the immediately political or ideological level.

The representation of society as the ideological discourse of the ruling class is but a bad compromise between two opposite, yet equally coherent, intellectual positions. According to the first, the organization of a society and its transformations are directed by the interests of the ruling class, or even more precisely, by the laws of capitalist economy. For the second, society is represented through the figure of a struggle between class forces for the control of historicity, that is, of the general cultural orientations of the society.

The first position posits the existence of a system defined by capitalist exploitation but socially manifested through the internal logic of the dominant system. This conception must face two objections. First, we must remember that although there most certainly exists an internal logic of class economic domination, nothing forces us to say that this logic rules completely over the working of society. To recognize the existence of capitalist power does not *ipso facto* require that we assert that it is total, that the State is but the agent of the dominant class, and that workers cannot lead social movements capable of overthrowing or of limiting this power. It is true that the dominant class always tends to oppose order (with which it identifies) to deviance (to which it reduces all those that oppose it), but it is even truer that a society must be analyzed as a confrontation among projects by classes contending for the direction of, and right to direct, historicity. To say that society is but a system of domination is tantamount to denying the existence, and the very possibility, of social movements; such a position can only be that of the ideology of a ruling elite concerned either with the preservation of its power or with accession to power by relying upon the crisis of the previous system rather than the challenges of dominated classes.

The second objection rejects the idea of such a complete independence of the economic order because economic and political facts are historically intertwined. Even those who speak of "State monoply capitalism" acknowledge the impossibility of defining a purely economic power because the State plays an essential role in their conception.

These two objections have such power that few people today defend the idea of a purely economic logic of domination independent of the exercise of political power and of ideological manipulation (propaganda, advertizing, cultural conditioning). How could one not see that the farther one goes in this direction, the more the ruling class appears as an actor and not as the mere bearer of the laws of an economic system?

In the central capitalist societies, the image of society as ideological discourse is so contrary to observable facts that one must look for the hidden reasons for its influence. It is nothing more than a replica of the utopia of the ruling class as it identifies its own interests with social evolution as a whole at a time when social struggles appropriate to the new forms of class domination have not developed. The value of the identification of social organization with dominant ideology is to reveal the latter's class nature and to denounce its favorite mask, that of the "end of ideology." Historically, the role of such an ideology critique has been entirely positive, following two decades of triumph for the ideology of the dominant class. But if it is necessary to criticize this ideology, it is imperative that it not be on its ground, and therefore that one not reduce social and cultural organization to a discourse; on the contrary, one must rediscover, directly or indirectly, the presence of social conflicts.

In its beginnings, American industrial sociology, though generally adopting a conservative outlook, gave a very good example of ideology critique by showing that the actual behavior of workers did not conform to Taylor's image of it, that the workers' response to financial stimulants was to slow down instead of increasing their production. The same type of analysis can be usefully applied to schools in order to understand the phenomenon of dropping out, as well as to many other areas of social life. Rebellions, rejections, retreats, flights, silences, aggressions, perversions of social or cultural instruments or their misappropriation—all these phenomena indicate the presence of oppositional forces, just as conflicts, ideologies, and negotiations do. For a brief period of time it has been useful to simply question the hold of the ruling class and elites over the whole of social practices. But, quite rapidly, it becomes apparent that this type of critique risks falling prey to the very illusions it is leveled against. It is not true that society is unidimensional and integrative and that it can be fought only from the outside or from the outer periphery. Social movements as much as the attacks on the international organization of the capitalist economy have revealed the fragility, the contradictions, and the conflicts present in this dominant order once believed to be so powerful, so much in charge of itself, and so assured of the reproduction of its profits and its privileges.

A sociology of action stands at the far side of this type of approach. Of course there are mechanisms for the reproductions of social domination. But, in the first instance, what is reproduced is never entirely reducible to a class domination. It is rather the decay of a class power into a coalition of privileges, more or less directly backed by a State that is against the people. And in the second instance, such a reproduction matches completely the production of class relations and conflicts only in special cases, those of totalitarianism on one side, and of conservative decadence on the other. There is nothing to warrant the assertion that the great capitalist countries presently belong wholly to either of these sides.

Taking Social Classes as Protagonists

Social classes are not only categories with unequal resources or opportunities. The ruling class presides over historicity, that is, over the set of means whereby a society, instead of merely reproducing itself, produces its own existence and its meaning. The societies studied by sociology have the capacity to distance themselves from themselves through knowledge, through investment, and through the representation of their own creativity. It would be artificial, however, to speak simplistically of a society acting upon itself. This type of action presupposes a dividing of the society, and that can be undertaken only by one part of the society upon the whole. A society that keeps on reproducing itself can be a community, whereas a society endowed with historicity, with the capacity to transform itself, is necessarily divided into a superior class, which manages accumulation, and a lower class, which suffers the witholdings managed and utilized by the former.

The notion of class has also a more specific historical signification. It makes its appearance in the social thought of modern times, especially in Scotland, in the eighteenth century, blossoms in the Europe of capitalist industrialization, and is now spreading into all the regions of the world, where new forms of industrialization directed by national or foreign bourgeoisies are springing up. Where does this historical privilege come from? From the fusing of the following three sets of facts during the period of capitalist industrialization.

First, class relations themselves as they obtain — under different forms, before the rise of industrial society as well as after it. Second, the coming into being of a metasocial order of an "economic" nature during the industrial era. Social facts are taken to be determined by economic facts or relations, whereas in preindustrial capitalism this metasocial order is of a "political" nature. In these merchant societies, class relations have an economic dimension, as everywhere else, but classes are defined by the properly political field in which their relations are inscribed, so that classes are agents in civil or political struggles at the same time as economic categories. This dualism of nature obtains everywhere except in industrial societies in which the field of class relations has itself become economic. Third and last, the industrialization of Western Europe, and especially that of Great Britain, has been directed by national bourgeoisies, classes that may thus have been taken to be one of the terms in class relations and as the elite directing historical transformation. Class struggles in the strict sense of the term have been confused with struggles for the direction of the State. It is the historically defined conjunction of these three senses of classes that has given them the role of central protagonists of history, first proclaimed by bourgeois historians like Guizot and Tocqueville.

The paradox of the present situation is that the advances in the action that society exercises upon itself go on extending the field of class relations and therefore the usefulness of the concept, but at a time when classes are less and less the chief protagonists of history. This paradox is more apparent than real; the disappearance of the metasocial orders, the effect of which is to extend infinitely the field of class conflicts, also dissolves the second of the three components just described as part of the image of classes proper to industrial societies.

Furthermore, the generalization to the entire globe of industrial civilization results in a greater diversity of ruling elites, proliferating societies in which there are State and not bourgeois elites, which means that we no longer can identify a priori ruling class and ruling elite.

Indeed one of the most urgent tasks of a sociology of action is to discover class relations in the very places where the landscape is no longer dominated by classes as protagonists. The bourgeoisie and the proletariat are no longer everywhere the heroes of industrialization. The social classes of our day are no longer historically delineable and nameable figures, and this because they can be defined only by class relations broadly covered by the power of States and parties.

Confusing Structure and Change in Evolutionary Philosophy

To explain social facts by appealing to the designs of Providence or by invoking the sense of History is of the same nature. To be sure, in the second case, the metasocial order to which social facts are related is in motion instead of static. But both conceptions ultimately hold that social facts, that is, social relations, are not bearers of their own meaning and that this meaning comes from a higher order. When this order is conceived as a movement from the simple to the complex, from the transmitted to the acquired, from reproduction to change, social facts must be understood by their place in this process of increasing differentiation and secularization. At that point there is no difference between the concepts used in the analysis of social structure and those utilized to obtain knowledge of change. Modernization provides a simple illustration of this: a modern society is one in which roles are highly differentiated, instrumental rationality reigns, and so on. The analysis of a "modern" society makes use of notions that always invoke the opposite image of a "traditional" society. The theories of Talcott Parsons, the influence of which has been considerable for quite some time, are a good example of this evolutionism narrowly associated with a functionalist analysis of social organization.

From the point of view of this social philosophy, society is not defined by its action, its social relations, and its forms of social control. It is defined at a more basic level by its modernity or its traditionalism, by its place on the hierarchical scale that goes from community (*Gemeinschaft*) to society (*Gesellschaft*), from mechanical solidarity to an organized one, and so on.

At a more concrete level, the action of the great historical actors was similarly defined in historical terms. It was always a question of setting up the society of tomorrow, conceived less as different than as more advanced. The bourgeoisie thought that its role was to succeed to the aristocracy, and the proletariat was proclaimed to be charged by history with the task of taking up the bourgeoisie's succession.

As soon as one resolves to explain social realities only by social relations, relations between actors defined as a function of society's mode of intervention upon itself, sociology cannot be identified with an evolutionist philosophy of history. There are, on the one hand, forms of societal self-production, of historicity, and on the other, modes of passage from one society to another—though I would rather call it the passage from one historical action system to another. This is no attempt to set aside interest in social evolution; it is to distinguish first and foremost the analysis of systems of social relations from that of the modes of passage from one society to another. We must keep structure and genesis apart.

This separation is possible with the creation of a type of industrial society that deviated from the British model. In spite of important differences, both the French and the German experience in this area belong to the same category as the British one. The Soviet revolution, on the contrary, invented an altogether different path toward industrialization. Since then, "paths" have multiplied to such an extent that no one can give much credence to a superficial theory of convergence, as if all the roads were different but did lead to Rome, that is, to a certain general type of social organization.

We must speak at the same time of industrial society and of capitalist, socialist, or other paths to industrialization. It is high time to do away with these collective protagonists of history, the bulky presence of which was imposed on us by the nineteenth century. People speak only of civilizations or of modes of production. Against all evidence, people feel obliged to call our societies "capitalist," whereas they should be defined as industrial. There cannot be any sociology unless and until we get rid of these characters ruled by the meaning of History.

We must radically separate a type of society, industrial society, from a mode of development, industrialization, which in the West took on a generally capitalist guise. An industrial society is not defined by technologies but by class relations, by the capacity of a social category to transform the organization of labor and to appropriate the profits that result from this operation. And this happens equally in the Soviet Union and in the United States. On the other hand, societies industrialized by a national bourgeoisie or a national State, or by a revolutionary party, or by a foreign bourgeoisie, are deeply different from one another.

In an industrial society, the condition of workers is thus two-dimensional, with important differences between the two. The first is defined by the organization of labor, the second by employment insofar as it evidences more directly the nature of the ruling elite. In parallel fashion, in a capitalist society, one should not confuse completely the industrializers, who exert a class domination, and the capitalists in the strict sense of the term, who see actions as based much more on a market economy than on an industrial one.

The social thought of the industrial era elaborated three basic themes upon which sociological analysis was built up: the social system, social conflicts, and the cultural orientations of action. The names of Durkheim, Marx, and Weber, without being reducible to any single one of these themes, became their symbols. But these three themes were not yet organized among themselves. And that is because the society in which they arose did not conceive of itself as subject to an analysis that would emanate from it. It was still under the sway of two ideas that are opposed to the existence of sociology. The first is that the meaning of a social situation is to be sought outside it, in a metasocial world that some call values and others nature. Weber, wondering about the reasons for the economic and political success of the Western world, and thus forced to inquire into the causes of capitalism, rationalization, and secularization, called on the relation to values, religious ones in this case, and proceeded to see a tension between the ethics of belief and the ethics of responsibility in all collective action. Marx, even beyond the period of his youth, confined himself to the analysis of the capitalist system; he referred to basic needs, to use value, to an image of society freed of capitalist exploitation, all of which introduced a contradiction between nature and society, which was but the proletarian interpretation of a general dualism, of which Weber gave us the bourgeois version. Durkheim, finally, though he did more than anyone else to introduce the idea of society as system, made society into an essence, a force that imposes itself upon actors much more than what is at stake in the relationships among actors.

The second idea to stand in the way of the birth of sociological analysis in the true sense of the term is evolutionism and the philosophy of history it implies. For it, a society is defined by its place in an evolution, the meaning of which, always associated with some form of progress, played the role of central interpretative principle. The entire nineteenth century was characterized by dreams of modernity, of progress, and of the future.

Slowly, and with difficulty, the passage from social thoughts to sociological analysis is taking place. The latter is inconceivable without the contributions of Marx, Weber, and Durkheim, but it will not come into being without breaking from the two ideas I have just discussed, ideas that define the historical inscription of these thinkers within the culture of industrialization.

This transformation can occur only through great crises. We are still going through a difficult transition during which social thought can begin to decay more visibly than sociological analysis can come into existence. Each of the major themes appears to be undergoing a "desociologization." Those who speak in the name of social conflicts and of the Marxist tradition most often oppose the social order to what it excludes, and are thus brought back to utopias and the weaknesses of utopian socialism. Those who are most sensitive to problems of action or agency are often experts close to the powerful and the mighty, whose decision making and strategies they seek to orient. Finally, those who speak of social systems see them as reproduction and integration mechanisms rather than places of conflict and change.

The time has come to put sociology together again. What we call society is a system, but it is an action system. And action is not only decisions; it is a purposefulness of cultural orientations through conflictual social relations. Conflicts are neither contradiction nor rebellion but the social forms of historicity, of the production of society by itself. Slowly, on the far side of evolutionism, comes into being the analysis of societies convinced by a long period of expansions and crises, of atomic threats, totalitarianisms and revolutions, that they should discover themselves as the products of their own action and not as the manifestation of a human nature, a meaning of history, or some originary contradiction. Beyond the rivalries among schools of thought and the limitations of specialization, we are living the mutation of sociology.

Chapter 6
Social Movements: Particular Object or Central Problem of Sociological Analysis?

Can sociology, which is usually defined as the analysis of the functioning of the social system, be broadened to include the study of social movements? Or, on the contrary, must sociology be reconstructed around the the latter? Those who answer yes to the second question are in two separate camps. For some, one must first give up the idea of social system in order to acknowledge that everything is change and that social movements are the agents of change; for others, to the contrary, one must keep the idea of social system but one must reconstruct it on the basis of an analysis of social movements, of the cultural field in which they are located, and of the institutionalized forms of their conflicts.

Most of all, the empiricist illusion must be clearly rejected: it is impossible to define an object called "social movements" without first selecting a general mode of analysis of social life on the basis of which a category of facts called social movements can be constituted. Many purely empirical studies of conflicts exist, but frequently one does not quite know what they are talking about. Nevertheless, a good number of them provide excellent descriptions of certain determinate events.

But if one remains committed to the construction and analysis of general categories, one must recognize at the outset that at least three types of conflicts aim to transform one or more important objects of social and cultural organization. In order to achieve some clarity in terminology, I propose to call *collective behavior* those conflictual actions that can be understood as attempts to defend, to reconstruct, or to adapt a sick element of the social system, be it a value, a norm, an authority relation, or the society itself. It is in this sense that Neil

Smelser[1] has used the expression collective behavior. On the other hand, if conflicts are analyzed as mechanisms for changing decisions, and thus as factors of change or political forces in the broadest sense of the terms, I propose to speak of *struggles*. Finally, when conflictual actions seek to transform the relations of social domination that are applied to the principal cultural resources (production, knowledge, ethical rules), they will be called *social movements*. One may have preference for other terminological conventions; I have chosen these because they seem closest to present usage. What matters most here is to distinguish clearly between these three modes of constructing the realm of observable reality since the same conflict may belong to one, two, or even all three of these types. Sociological analysis cannot take the place of historical analysis, which grasps the specific complexity of the conflict.

Collective Behavior

A great many conflicts appear to be best analyzed as effects of the decomposition of a threatened social system and as efforts to reconstruct it. For example: some immigrants create a homogeneous community; progressively it becomes differentiated, with some getting richer, others poorer, and still others marrying outside the group. As a result, the community is under threat. A messiah or a prophet appears then to restore ancient ways, that is, the homogeneity and integration of the community. This circumstance is important in so-called reform movements, and even in revolutions such as the English one of the seventeenth century, in addition to the messianic and fundamentalist movements I have just mentioned. Similarly, an important part of organized labor activity lies in mounting a defense of qualification standards and pay scales against the consequences of a technical change or an alteration of the market or a decision of management. These examples show that the space for such behavior grows ever smaller in rapidly changing societies that are highly diversified and whose degree of homogenization and integration is therefore lower than that of traditional societies. In industrial societies, collective behavior is defined more often by the effort to master change and orient the future than by a will to preserve the past or return to it.

However, for some time now, the reforming and integrating type of behavior seems to be recovering a far from negligible importance, owing to the fact that "modern" values, such as change, growth, and development, long considered as untouchable as progress or the natural movement of history, have been called into question, notably in dependent or colonized countries in which imported modernization and industrialization have made a shambles of traditional social and cultural organization. Such movements, which were already visible in Asia, Latin America, and Africa at the height of nineteenth-century colonial expansion, have recently developed considerably, as witnessed by the success of

Khomeinism in Iran. In the Communist world as well, national consciousness is again on the rise, whereas in the "first world," the Western industrialized nations see the spread of themes of community and identity with actions that indeed correspond to what I have called collective behavior.

The signification of collective behavior is necessarily far removed from the consciousness of its actors, since it is defined in terms of the functioning of the social system and not in terms of the representations or of the projects of the actors (in the same way as suicide is defined in Durkheim's analysis). That is why collective behavior is essentially heteronomous, oriented by external economic or political constraints, or directed by a leader who is the head of a sect or of a fundamentalist movement that identifies with the order to be restored.

Struggles

Thus the reference to society, to the social order, tends to be invoked more and more in our countries in order to define actions that are not linked to change but rather those that combat it in the name of an older or of a newer order. This leads us quite far from what we spontaneously call "movement." Hence the natural tendency of both participants in, and observers of, these social conflicts in industrial societies to insist upon the conflicts and mechanisms of change. But this very definition does not have the meaning it had in the nineteenth century, when the labor movement was the actor in the most important conflicts and appeared to represent new values, those of progress and industrialization, while it fought against the social forms of appropriation.

Today, this central role of a social movement as chief agent of historical transformations is put into doubt, and it is hard to see what unifies all these numerous conflicts that do not invoke some central values, do not combat a dominant power, but seek only to modify some relations of power or some specific decision-making mechanisms. Under such circumstances agents of change cannot be defined globally in the name of some "direction of history." Even more so perhaps than in the world of labor, urban life provides the best evidence of this passage from central social movements to particular struggles. The numerous studies of contemporary urban struggles show that these consist most often in limited actions, aimed at landlords or administrative authorities in order to achieve better housing conditions. A growing number of urban struggles tend to become akin to what has earlier been called collective behavior, in defending a threatened environment, as, for example, in the eventually successful struggle waged in Madrid to safeguard the historic center of the city.

These struggles gain in importance as they seek a more direct access to decision-making power, that is, when they become associated with a political party. This is why in several large industrial countries, social-democratic parties (both revolutionary and reformist) have tightly linked social struggles to political action, and indeed subordinated them to it, with the fundamental objective of seizing power.

Social Movements

To speak of collective behavior is to look at conflicts as responses to a situation that needs be apprehended in itself, that is, in terms of the integration or disintegration of a social system defined by a principle of unity. To speak of struggles, on the other hand, implies a strategic conception of social change. Struggles are not responses but initiatives whose action does not end up in, and indeed does not even aim at, constructing a social system. This explains why the idea of struggles is more or less directly associated with the representation of society as either market or battlefield. Between competition and war there are many other conflictual strategies, but none of them refers to the idea of a social system defined by values, norms, and institutions.

By contrast, the passage from struggles to social movements reestablishes the relation between collective action and social system, but it inverts it. Let us start with an example. In a factory there emerges a movement to fight against unequal wages for workers with comparable qualifications (an example of simple collective behavior) or to increase the influence of the wage earners on decisions that affect their working conditions (a case of struggle). The very organization of the business itself, however, does not represent the result of pure technical rationality, nor is it the direct outcome of an ever shifting relation of forces. It is inherent in the industrial sphere for the control of the holders of capital to have extended from the sale of products to the working conditions of producers gathered in a factory and subjected, in authoritarian fashion, to a given collective organization of work. The workers' action is directed against this domination and is meant to give them, or the whole of the collectivity, control over the organization of labor and over the resources created by industrial activity.

A social movement thus defined is in no way a response to a social situation. On the contrary, it is the social situation that is the outcome of the conflict between social movements fighting for control over cultural models, over historicity, and this conflict may lead to a break up of the political system or to institutional reforms. A social movement is a conflictual action through which cultural orientations, a field of historicity, are transformed into forms of social organization defined by general cultural norms and by relations of social domination.

A rapidly failing notion of society and an ever weaker classical sociology force us to choose between either a sociology of pure change, in which the notion of struggle occupies an important place, or a sociology of action, which rests upon the notions of cultural models and social movements. A large part of the great debates in sociology can be understood as competition, conflict, or compromise between these three orientations.

Classical sociology was born in countries such as Great Britain, Germany, the United States, and France; these constituted political, economic, and cultural ensembles that were so distinct that one could speak not only of nationally defined societies but also of nationally defined social actors (organized labor or the entrepreneurs, for example). This is no longer true: a great many social actors defend their interests in markets or in competitive, or even conflictual, arenas that are more likely to be defined by a technology or an economic conjuncture, by strategic conflicts or cultural trends of international scope, than by an overall national reality. No social movement today can identify with the whole of the conflicts and the forces for social change in a national society. As a result, the field of struggles becomes more and more autonomous in relation to the action of social movements (although this trend could be reversed in other social situations), and collective behavior tends more and more toward what I have called *social antimovements*. For indeed the dissociation of the mode of economic development from the forms of functioning of economic and social systems over most of this planet has provoked a massive resurgence in social conflicts and collective actions carried out in the name of the social and cultural integration of a community. This dissociation among social movements, struggles, and collective behavior protects a sociology centered on the analysis of social movements from the danger of turning itself into a philosophy of history. Not only is it no longer possible to locate sociological analysis within an evolutionist representation that led from the traditional to the modern, from mechanical solidarity to an organic one, from community to society, but the very disappearance of the hegemony of the central capitalist countries over the whole of the world prohibits the identification of their historicity and their specific social movements with a universal history, the stages of which would be mandatory steps in the development of all countries.

We must break with the classical idea that identifies creativity with its works, and a historicity defined as reason and progress with mastery over nature by science and technology. If we effect this break, we must reintroduce into sociological analysis another conception of the subject, one that stresses the distance between creation and works, between consciousness and practices. For if it is true that cultural models turn into social practices through conflicts between opposed social movements, it must also be the case that they disengage themselves from these practices in order to become models of investment and for the creation of norms—all of which implies reflexivity, distanciation, and, to use a term deeply rooted in the cultural tradition of the West, *consciousness*. In some epochs, social thought insists more, within historicity, upon economic investment and the production of knowledge; at other times, it is more sensitive to the creation and transformation of ethical models, and then it grants more importance to distanciation than to investment. Actually, these are complementary moves, and it would be as dangerous to fall into moral philosophy as into the philosophy of history.

The notion of social movement is inseparable from that of class. But what opposes social movement to class is the fact that the latter can be defined as a situation, whereas a social movement is an action, the action of a subject, that is, of an actor who calls into question the social form of historicity. For too long, the study of the labor movement was reduced to the study of capitalism, its crises and conjuncture. In even more extreme fashion, studies of the social and national movements of the Third World have remained beholden to analyses of imperialism and of the world economic system, to the point where the rise of mass movements seemed impossible, and this in turn led to the privileging of armed struggle, be it by guerrillas or in the form of mass military struggle led by a revolutionary party.

As soon as any recourse to a metasocial principle is eschewed and, as a consequence, the idea of a contradiction between society and nature is also rejected, it becomes necessary to conceive of classes as actors caught in conflicts and not in contradictions. In order to mark this important change, it is preferable, then, to speak of social movements rather than social classes. *A social movement is the action, both culturally oriented and socially conflictual, of a social class defined by its position of domination or dependency in the mode of appropriation of historicity, of the cultural models of investment, knowledge, and morality, toward which the social movement itself is oriented.*

Social movements are never isolated from other types of conflicts. The workers' movement, which is directed against the social power of the masters of industry, is inseparable from the claims and pressures aimed at increasing the influence of labor unions in economic, social, and political decisionmaking. But its existence is marked by the presence of nonnegotiable elements in negotiations, and thus it becomes impossible for a union that is the bearer of the workers' movement to carry out a purely instrumental action, in terms of costs and advantages. What has been called market unionism does not belong to the workers' movement, hence the development of forms of behavior aimed at rupture: wildcat strikes, absenteeism, slow-downs, acts of violence or of sabotage, all of which manifest the repressed presence of a workers' movement within market unionism or within unions with overly institutionalized claims and demands.

This initial observation can be broadened. Representative democracy is, properly speaking, a system in which political actors depend on the social actors whom they represent, while preserving some measure of autonomy so that they act both in terms of their position in decision systems and as emissaries of interest groups or of movements. Public opinion views this phenomenon with irony when the double discourse of the representatives is highlighted, as when what they say in their district is juxtaposed with their statements during parliamentary committee meetings. A political debate can thus be what I call a struggle and, at the same time, convey a social movement.

Similarly, the workings of an organization cannot be analyzed only in terms of relations of authority. Decisions made by management can also be explained by the policies of the board of directors or even those of the shareholders, whereas the behavior of the workers or of the white-collar workers is largely dominated by their view of a general conflict of interests that exceeds the frame of their professional existence.

We have gotten too used to speaking of the passage of the class "in itself" to the class "for itself," of an accepted situation to a consciousness that is raised with the transition to political action. Actually, there is no class "in itself"; there is no class without a class consciousness. But a distinction must be made between a social class consciousness—that is, a social movement that is always present, even if in diffuse ways, as soon as there is conflict over the social appropriation of the key cultural resources—and a political class consciousness, which ensures the translation of a social movement into political action. An action directed against social domination is never reduced to a strategy with respect to political power.

The definition of social movements given thus far presents them as agents in the structural conflicts of a social system. But don't we find social movements at the very level of cultural models and not at the level of their social utilization? Furthermore, must the analysis of social movements limit itself to a synchronic perspective or must it extend to the realm of change? Cultural innovation, and resistance to it, cannot constitute by themselves a social movement, for the latter combines by definition a reference to the field of culture with the consciousness of a social relation of domination. But a cultural conflict may well include a social dimension, and ultimately always does so: there is such a thing as a cultural model in itself wholly independent of the mode of domination that is exerted upon it. Between a purely cultural conflict, such as that within a scientific or an artistic community, and the cultural expression of a directly social conflict, there lies a vast field occupied by cultural movements defined equally by their opposition to an old or a new cultural model and by an internal conflict between two modes of social use of the new cultural model.

The most important cultural movement today is that of women. On the one hand, it is opposed to traditional women's conditions and thus overturns our image of the subject; on the other hand, it is divided between two tendencies that actually represent two opposed social forces: a liberal tendency, which fights for equality and draws the upper social layers (it is more interesting to claim access to the practice of medicine, or to the Senate, than to manual labor), and a radical tendency, which fights more for specificity than for equality and is in fact suspicious of the traps of equality. The radical tendency fights a domination that is both social and sexual by linking the action of women to that of the proletariat, by denouncing specifically sexual domination, or finally by setting a relational conception of social life closer to the biopsychological experience of women against a technocratic conception of male origin.

Cultural movements are particularly important at the beginning of a new historical period when political actors are not yet representative of new social movements or claims, and when the transformation of the cultural field calls forth fundamental debates about knowledge, economic investment, and mores.

Alongside social movements in the strict sense of the term and cultural movements, or more exactly sociocultural movements, we must recognize the existence of *sociohistorical movements*. The latter are not located within a field of historicity, as social movements are, but in the passage from one type of society to another – a passage of which industrialization is the most important form. The new element here is that the conflict is organized around the management of development, and that as a result the dominant actor is not a ruling class defined by its role in a mode of production, but a ruling *elite*, that is, a group that leads development and historical change and is defined above all by the ruling of the *State*. A sociohistorical movement may be associated with an industrializing State, or it may be opposed to it. The two camps have in common the fact that they want development and modernization, but one wants to reinforce the capacity of the State to make investments and to mobilize resources whereas the other appeals to the nation and to popular participation.

There is a kinship between these three types of movements, which explains why some, having located themselves in a revolutionary tradition, have affirmed the fundamental unity of the workers' movement with that of the national liberation movements and the women's liberation movement. But it is more important to underline the deep differences that separate them and prevent them from unifying. Thus the Third World is dominated by the constant opposition of class movements with nationalist movements, and not by their union; both types of movement can be unified only under the aegis of a nationalist revolutionary party and always at the cost of the destruction of both of its constituents, with the party that absorbs them turning authoritarian. Similarly, the attempts to bring together the workers' movement and the women's movement have come against such difficulties that most of the radical women militants have removed themselves from any political or union action that seemed in their opinion to be deaf to the specific demands of women.

Action, Order, Crisis, and Change

The set of problems we have considered in this chapter constitutes one of the large "areas" of sociological analysis, namely that of social action. But there are other "areas" as well. The specificity of social action lies in the fact that it is always analyzed in terms of unequal social relations (power, domination, influence, authority). But social relations are never completely "open"; we have already said that they close up, that they turn into a *social order* upheld by agencies of social and cultural control, and, ultimately, by the power of the State. This social order can also deteriorate into *crisis,* especially when its stability enters into conflict with the changes in the environment. In this way, the area of crisis is added to those of social action and of order as parts of sociological analysis. Finally, still in the same type of society, namely industrial society, social relations and orders are constantly undergoing a process of *change*. Can the analysis of social movements get out of its specific area and enter those of order, crisis, and change?

Any claim to hegemony by the sociology of social movements must be rejected. The latter does not govern either directly or completely the study of order (that is, also that of repression and exclusion), nor those of crisis or change. What prevails presently is a state of affairs in which the sociology of social movements appears to be one of the weakest and least elaborated realms of sociological analysis. Yet one cannot wholly embrace a total methodological pluralism that would end up by completely dismembering social reality and its analysis.

The entry of a sociology of social movements into what I have called the area of order appears nearly impossible — so opposed are these two intellectual orientations. For the past twenty years, if not longer, from Marcuse to Foucault, and Althusser to Bourdieu, a whole set of reflections, quite differentiated among themselves to be sure, has achieved widespread influence in the social sciences by claiming that contemporary society is subjecting itself to ever stricter control and surveillance in such a way that social life is nothing more than the system of the signs of an unrelenting domination. In this way any social movement that would be more than a rebellion quickly shunted into the margins of a "unidimensional society" is excluded. In point of fact, the increasing hold of society upon itself risks making public space disappear altogether rather than extending it, by giving the central power the means for intervening in all aspects of social organization, cultural life, and individual personality. It is true though that the lively protest activity of the sixties has been supplanted by a lasting weakening of social movements.

These pessimist conceptions have proven the more influential as studies on education or on social work have demonstrated their powerlessness to fight against social inequalities and even their tendency to reinforce them through mechanisms of selection. And so today the sociology of social movements does not clash so much with a sociology of institutions or of the social system, themselves weakened by cultural and social crises, as with the sociology of the State ideological apparatuses. Hence it becomes important for the sociology of social movements to gain entry into this apparently hostile territory.

Let us begin by stressing that it is possible now to indicate the limitations of the theses that present schools or social work as institutions incapable of bringing significant change in social inequalities, theses that imply that educators or social workers can never really be actors. To such inordinate claims, one can counterpose a number of studies[2] that show clearly that inequality obtains only partially at the outset and that it actually develops within the school system and by it. It would be more fitting, then, to exchange the impersonal responsibility of the "system" for the individual and collective responsibilities of educators. All that allows a limiting of the school form in favor of active learning in which the child is not only a pupil but an individual recognized in the plurality of the social roles he or she is called on to play (including those in class) contributes to the reduction of inequality of opportunity.[3]

Second, order never prevails absolutely; we may speak of ideological control, manipulation, and alienation, but what we actually have is physical repression, violence, and rebellion, reduced to degraded forms. Just as there is never total silence in the world of slavery or in the concentration camps because there always subsists some resistance and therefore some direct repression, so behind the facade of order there always survive social relations of domination and protest. We have recently had an exceptional demonstration of this phenomenon, one that shattered the far too easily accepted idea that totalitarian regimes have the capacity of reaching such a stability that they can reduce to impotence or completely marginalize any opposition: almost overnight in Poland, the official order crumbled and social life was born again, like Lazarus emerging from the tomb. In a few weeks, actors, debates, conflicts, and negotiations rose on all sides, proof of the powerlessness of the regime save for recourse to State violence. Similarly in other seemingly silent countries, a weakening or a crisis of the repressive regime can free up a social life that remained alive in spite of persecutions and the reign of deadening official speech; is it not remarkable to see social life rise up again in so many places where it appeared to have been crushed: in Brazil; in Chile, Poland, Romania; even in China? What is most moving about Solzhenitsyn's *Gulag Archipelago* is not so much the description of the horror of the Gulag (which was already known) as the fact that he makes us hear voices that extermination has not silenced.

If we consider analyses conducted in terms of crisis, we can see that they are more open to the idea of social movement than are those that rest upon the notion of order. Let us take a most current example: the social effects of unemployment. The numerous studies on this subject tend far too often to speak of nothing but anomie and marginality. It was far more difficult in the thirties to satisfy oneself with talk of the psychological effects of unemployment and of marginalization; during that decade the United States experienced hunger marches, while in Europe the Fascist movements fed on unemployment. Was it possible in the nineteenth century to separate completely what was then called the "dangerous class" from the "working class"? Closer to us, was it possible but a few years ago to take the small group of Black Panthers in Oakland as just a gang of Black marginals? And similarly today are the young immigrants of Les Minguettes simply "marginals" or also the crafters of a nascent social movement? To be sure, crises bring forth more often behavior of deviant hyperconformism[4] (sects and other forms of social antimovements) than social movements; but in every case the inadequacy of analyses conducted in terms of crisis and social decomposition is apparent.

Let us finally consider behavior linked to change. It tends to be so close to that of social movements that it has often been confused with the latter and we must take pains to mark the distance between them. The space of social change is actually doubly sloped: on one side it leans to social relations and to the effects of the institutionalization of conflicts, and therefore of reforms, whereas on the other it leads toward development, that is, toward the passage from one cultural and societal field to another. It is this necessary decomposition of an artificially constituted ensemble that makes the entry of the sociology of social movements possible in the area of social life.

An important notion here is that of *reinforcement* because it is usable in all cases. Observable behavior may indeed be explained as a response to integration or to exclusion, to crisis or to change, but such explanations always leave out an important residue which can be analyzed only as a set of indirect effects of either the coming into being or, on the contrary, of the absence of social movements. Where conflict does not ferment, we have the reign of apparent unity or order as well as violence and withdrawal. This notion of reinforcement presents the advantage of respecting the autonomy of the modes of analysis that correspond more directly to one of the areas of social life, while keeping the existence of general principles of analysis. Let us add that when we speak of reinforcement we do not mean to say that an explanation in terms of social movements gives a better account than others of all of historical reality. The weakening of many recent conflicts, notably of the ecological movement, provides ample proof to the contrary, namely that they aren't energetic enough to develop into social movements and that a determinant role is played within them by behavior of another type. We should even acknowledge that it is possible for anyone to organize the whole of sociological analysis in terms of social system, integration, and crisis. But when one seeks to analyze vast and complex social ensembles, and to determine the nature of the social forces that can transform them, the notions of historicity and of social movement must take center stage.

There are many who think that our society is unable to produce new social movements, because any such movements would be swallowed up in the irresistible rise of managerial and integrating States, because an enriched society is supposed to be able to absorb all tensions, or because social movements are supposed to be products of accumulating societies with rapid change whereas we are heading back toward a balanced society. On the contrary, to seek to understand the new social movements is to defend another representation of our society and of its future. According to this representation, we are entering into a new mode of production, which, by giving rise to new conflicts, will give birth to new social movements, extending and diversifying social space but also perhaps extending forms of domination and of social control that will reach deeper and be even more adept at manipulation.

Chapter 7
The Two Faces of Identity

The theme of identity is presently gaining in importance in the social sciences. It is a social fact, the manifestation of a general sensitivity on the part of a particular professional group to this ethical and cultural theme. How can one fail to establish a relation between such an interest taken by psychologists and sociologists and the appearance, or development, all over the world and in nearly all areas of social life, of claims, social or national movements that appeal for a defense of personal or collective identity? This should not lead us to surrender to ideology and be content to express our opinion about the opinion of others; we cannot forget, however, that our main task is to reflect upon social facts and to extract from them ideas and instruments of analysis. For sociologists, the starting point is obvious: the appeal to identity is an appeal to a nonsocial definition of the social actor. For them, actors are defined by the social relations in which they are inscribed. This is the definition of role, which applies equally to class or interpersonal relations. The appeal to identity is thus first of all a rejection of social roles, or, more precisely, a refusal of the social definition of the roles that must be played by the actor.

In the case of most societies, the appeal to identity relies upon a metasocial guarantor of social order, such as the essence of humanity or, more simply, one's belonging to a community defined by certain values or by a natural or historical attribute. But in our society the appeal to identity seems more often to refer not to a metasocial guarantor but to an infrasocial and natural force. The appeal to identity becomes an appeal, against social roles, to life, freedom, and creativity. Finally, the State itself appeals to identity against social roles, and attempts to impose the idea of a unity above all forms of particular belongings. A national State, for example, appeals to citizenship and, through it, to patriotism against all social, professional, and geographical differences. The individual or collective appeal to identity is thus the obverse of social life. Whereas the latter is a network of relations, the locus of identity is all at once that of individuals, communities, and States.

The Great Overturning

We have become used to looking at modern history as the difficult but irreversible passage from particularisms to universalism. Has it not been the aim of our educational system for quite some time now to take children from their original environment in order to open broader possibilities for them or to put them in touch with facts, thoughts, and works believed to have universal or exemplary scope? We are still living on the inheritance of the Enlightenment. In the countries of the West, the Left, in particular, has constantly opposed the forces of tradition and the domination of local luminaries; in fact if it constantly called on the State, it was to use its power, which it identified with that of collective will against the masters and holders of tradition.

Many other examples could be given, but these suffice to recall that until recently we analyzed our own historical experience by means of the idea of progress, and we identified the latter with the passage from tradition to innovation, belief to reason, identity to democracy, that is, with a mechanism of change. Some are even ready to go further and believe that our societies should be analyzed exclusively from the point of view of change, giving up all effort to define what is called social structures, and therefore any attempt at typology and even more so at representing historical evolution.

This general conception has taken two particular forms. One is the liberal version which I have just invoked in its most extreme form. Historical evolution would then be the passage from closed societies to open ones, from societies of control to societies of freedom. The other version conceives of this evolution as the passage from absolute power to democracy, that is, as the reduction of power to the results of social relations, through the advances of representative democracy within the political or the economic order. These two conceptions entail completely opposite consequences, but both are led to exclude the idea of identity from their ideology.

It is astonishing to see how quickly this general conception has been breaking down or is being rejected. The crucial fact here is the rapidly growing role of subordinate societies struggling against their dependence or against colonization. Whereas a century ago only the "central" societies seemed to have a history, contemporary history is ever more dominated by policies of national and social liberation. The nineteenth century in Europe was marked by the dream of the withering away of the State, of the triumph of civil society and of democracy; the twentieth century is dominated by the resurgence of States struggling against the domination of hegemonic powers. These States appeal to an identity against a domination with universalist claims. Nationalism, which to Europeans appeared to be more and more archaic and the source of destructive wars, returns today in "progressive" guise. The universalist and progressive values of Europe tend to appear increasingly as ideological instruments for its domination over the rest of the world and therefore as instruments of very particularist interests.

Within the industrialized societies themselves, the idea of progress is held in check, especially when it is expressed as the belief in the indefinite growth of production. Instead of looking at ourselves as the lords and masters of nature, we feel that we face choices that are not reducible to quantitative transformations but rather are concerned with elaborating different relations between human beings and their environment as well as among human beings themselves. We are replacing the idea of indefinite progress with that of a choice, by particular collectivities, of equally particular life-styles and social organization.

Finally, whereas the appeal to the State seemed to be universalist, to be a force opposing traditional local dominations, the development of the power of the State — within the realm of culture, (in particular that of information) as well as in the economic realm — leads us to oppose to this growing power which risks becoming totalitarian, the resistance of local collectivities and even that of private life.

At an even more general level, we are replacing in our hypercomplex societies the idea that efficacy is tied to homogeneity and uniformity with the opposite notion that it is linked to the quantity of information created or held in the system, that is, to its diversity. We no longer think that it enriches us to abandon local languages and cultures so that we may all partake of the universalist image of English or French culture; on the contrary, we are more inclined to believe that the richness of the whole is made up of its diversity and flexibility.

We are faced, then, with a difficult choice. Few are those, in our societies at least, who completely give up what could be called the progressive image of history and who do not view the countries of the world as separated by qualitative differences. Even fewer are those who wish for a general return to the past and who have an entirely regressive image of progress. At the same time, however, the appeal to specificity, to difference, to nationalism, to all forms of identity, is gaining ground. We are thus faced with nearly complete confusion. To take but one example, from the political realm: a Left and an extreme Left of revolutionary orientation have supported movements of national liberation and States that appealed to identity, and, like the Egyptian communists under Nasser or the Iranian Left after the fall of the Shah, later find themselves in the prisons of the very ruler they formerly acclaimed. The confusion becomes more extreme when the nationalist themes, which seemed to have gone over to the Left, suddenly return to their place of origin, that is, are assumed by a new Right which, in France, appeals to a French nationalism backed up by a specific cultural tradition and mobilized in the defense of what it views as its superiority.

This is where the social sciences can make an impact since social practices seem to carry contradictory meanings.

Crisis Behavior

We must begin by putting forward an explanation for the ambiguity of the notion of identity and of the ideas and movements that appeal to it. Social domination is today more diversified and reaches deeper, though less brutally, than in earlier types of society. It is inherent in technocratic apparatuses to be able to produce demand for the supply they control, to elicit needs, and thus to intervene directly in culture, in the definition of values, as opposed to intervening solely in relations of production or in the distribution of goods. This is why a defense against this domination cannot be mounted by appealing to a community or to a professional craft, as was true in industrial or preindustrial societies. And so the defense efforts appeal more and more to that which is least social in human beings. They call on nature, in the collective sphere, and on the body, the unconscious, interpersonal relations, desire, in the individual sphere. But such a defense stands no chance of turning into a social movement, or more simply of producing a capability for collective action, unless it links up with a counteroffensive movement, in the same way that a defense of labor life, culture, and craft was able to feed into a labor movement only insofar as it associated itself with a counteroffensive movement that called for the factories to be turned over to the workers and for the creation of a society of producers. This counteroffensive is sometimes signified by the slogan of self-management. Since the dominated can no longer draw support from something they have gained, they demand above all the right and capacity to determine for themselves the choices that affect their social and personal lives. This counteroffensive action is at a far remove from the idea of identity. It is directly political; it appeals to the notions of self-determination and of social and cultural democracy. The contemporary social and political scene is thus occupied, on the side of those who do not hold power, both by an appeal to an identity defined more and more as natural and less and less as social and by ever more direct political demands that are expressed not in terms of identity but in those of social relations and power. This leads to the conclusion that the appeal to identity must be defined as defensive behavior divorced from any counteroffensive behavior; hence its ambiguity. The appeal to identity is truly a force of social struggle since defense constitutes half of action. But at the same time it is the destruction of a capacity for social action inasmuch as it cuts the defensive from the counteroffensive. This appeal to identity is thus both the first stage in the formation of a social movement and the failure to effect a passage to the second stage, that is, to the actual production of social movements. We must therefore presently define the features of the appeal to identity when it is the first stage in the formation of a social movement, as opposed to when it constitutes a barrier to such a formation. Actually we will be led to distinguish between three and not two instances, introducing between the two we have described an intermediate category in which the appeal to identity does constitute the formation of a movement of collective action but one directed more against external rather than internal domination, against a State rather than a ruling class.

Defensive Behavior

A cry is being sounded in preindustrialized regions. It is a cry to defend an identity, a type of production, and a mode of life. One finds, of course, the leading citizens and other privileged persons in the forefront of this movement for the defense of a collective identity since they are its chief articulators as well as its principal beneficiaries. In France a great many traditionalist regional movements have developed, in Normandy and in Brittany particularly before World War II, but even today in many regions. One must be especially careful in distinguishing these movements of regional defense from those in favor of regional development, and even more so from movements of national liberation. In other countries, religious sects or messianic movements can be examples of movements rising to the defense of a utopian collectivity threatened by social differentiation and secularization. In such instances, as in many others, the appeal to identity appears to be particularly linked to the defense of traditional elites.

A second type of appeal to identity is far more dramatic. Any collectivity beset by a severe crisis tends to substitute for its internal conflicts the opposition of inside and outside, of internal integration and an external threat reinforced by traitors operating within the community who will be treated as scapegoats. Nazism, even more so than Italian Fascism, appealed to an identity constructed as both national and populist (*volkisch*) and bringing about the identification of a natural being with a collective will, a race with a history. Similarly, the New Right appeals to biology in order to ground its nationalism; in other words, it appeals to the supposed natural superiority of those who have been the masters of the world and therefore ought to retain this mastery, and to their cultural identity, which they are in the process of losing either because they are falling into the trap of hedonism or because they are allowing themselves to be conquered by new empires.

A third type of behavior in the defense of identity has been analyzed more recently. For some observers, who place themselves in the lineage of Tocqueville, the appeal to identity is but a particular form of the massification and destructuring of a society ever more subjected to the absolute power of the State. Instead of representing a gain, identity, for them, would be a surrender of the autonomy and of the specificity of the social actor as well as the acceptance of centrally generated manipulations. Christopher Lasch has spoken of a narcissistic personality in order to define this breakup of a personality constantly searching for an identity defined outside real social relations, that is, in domains, and under conditions, set by manipulatory powers. Identity then turns into a discontinuous series of identifications with models produced by mass culture.

Populism

The appeal to identity is no longer defensive and becomes a force for bringing into being a collective action when it is not opposed to social change but is issued against a domination that is viewed as foreign. Indeed one of the more momentous political phenomena of our times is the rise of such identity, or fundamentalist, movements. The various revolutions, from the French to the Soviet, have constantly appealed to liberating forces against an Ancien Régime. Today's antirevolutions—the most important of which is that which brought down the Shah in Iran, and other examples of which abound outside the Islamic realm and can even be found at our doorstep—are not opposed to an Ancien Régime but to a bloodless revolution, that is, to a modernization imposed from the outside which overturns the older social and cultural organization. It is in the name of this older organization and its values that the people rise. The more populist the movement, the weaker the role of the national State, and the more extreme the fundamentalism, the more terrorist the action, whereas in both of the older instances of the French and the Soviet revolutions, the reign of terror was linked to the triumph of a Jacobin State over popular forces. The strength of this appeal to identity is correlated with the mode of foreign domination and with how direct and how complete that domination is. In no way does this type of appeal to identity lead to a liberation movement. Since it is at war with a State and a culture, it can only appeal to culture and State, in fact to an absolute or totalitarian State and to a repressive culture. When a socially defensive movement is not associated with a social counteroffensive, it can only bring about the reinforcing of the State or of community closure, that is, an identity that fundamentally rests upon exclusion.

Offensive Identity

Altogether different is the defensive appeal to identity that completes and reverses itself by turning into a set of claims, a pretext against the power that destroys not so much identity as the capacity for autonomous intervention by collectivities and individuals. Most of the social movements that coalesce in our societies can be analyzed as attempts to go from the defensive to the offensive, as forces working upon defensive identity.

What are often called nationality movements are, in part at least, efforts to transform and even to overturn movements for the defense of a traditional identity into movements for autonomous regional development or even into movements of national liberation. The case of the antinuclear movement is even clearer. It is true that it would not have come about without defense reactions, a defense of local collectivities threatened by large installations and by cultural as well as economic disruption, and a defense of populations that feel threatened in their physical, and even their genetic, identity. Studies have shown, however, that antinuclear action soon peters out if it stays at this level; it organizes and develops only when these defense reactions are integrated with an antitechnocratic critique that appeals to modernity against those who hold power, and it counterposes a mode of social organization and development to the one being advanced. Finally, the women's movement, which begins with a defensive appeal to identity, difference, specificity, and community, survives and grows in influence only insofar as it turns into a movement directed against a type of social power, into an action led by women but not only for them, against the power and the wealth identified with male power.

To the sociologist, identity is, then, no longer an appeal to a mode of being but the claim to a capacity for action and for change. It is defined in terms of choice and not in terms of substance, essence, or tradition. This process of definition cannot take place entirely within the framework of an appeal to identity. The latter can be only a constitutive part of a social movement that is defined by the combination of a defense of identity, an awareness of social conflict, and an appeal to the collective control of some cultural orientations and of the great means by which society produces itself. Thus the passage from defensive identity to offensive identity is as much the passage from one principle of action to the interdependence of several complementary principles. This is a difficult passage since it threatens actors, especially by dissociating different realms of their action as well as by introducing in almost necessary fashion a distance between the expressive basis of the action and its instrumental organization or its political strategy. That is why one can never identify a social movement with a claim of identity. The labor movement is never the working class, fully aware and organized. The defense of a region or of a nation is never the action of a people on the move. We are close to the most hidden form of the way in which the notion of identity intervenes in the sociological field. The appeal to identity is ultimately the defensive action of the social militant against the very conditions of that militant's collective action. Deep within every social movement there is always to be found a fundamentalist and communitarian tendency, which can be a democratic reminder originating in the ethics of conviction and directed against the "politicizing" of the action, but which can be as much, and more negatively, an overturning of the social movement and its transformation into a sectarian one. We see once more the ambiguity of identity which can both restore life to collective action and lock it up behind the walls of sectarianism.

Identity cannot be opposed to social participation and to the exercise of social roles; by the same token, it cannot be confused with them. In preindustrial societies, the appeal to identity was a call to the order that ruled the social sphere, no matter if this identity was conceived as religious, national, or class-based. Today, on the contrary, if identity is opposed to the organization of social life, it will be marginalized or manipulated by those who direct it. On the other hand, the appeal to identity can be considered a labor of democracy, an awareness of the effort by which the actors of a social system that exerts a great deal of power upon itself and that is engaged in ceaseless change attempt to determine for themselves the conditions within which their collective and personal life is produced.

Chapter 8
Change and Development

The analysis of social change presented conceptual difficulties for the social thought we have inherited. Not because its preoccupations were limited to that which exhibited stability but, quite to the contrary, because it rested upon the idea of *evolution*. As long as sociology retains this evolutionist orientation, it cannot conceive of social change because it cannot dissociate the analysis of the social system from that of change. Synchronic analysis occupies today a larger and more important space than does diachronic analysis, but not for reasons of principle but because it has broken with evolutionism and has thus made a theory of change possible. This idea has been accepted only very recently, especially in the lands where historical thought had been most successful: Germany, France, England, and Italy. For quite some time, there was sounded in these countries an almost national opposition to the themes of functionalist sociology which then appeared to be identified with American thought. A wrong battle if there ever was one, since Parsons had indicated very clearly that his analysis of society was grounded in an evolutionist conception and rested upon the idea, inherited from the nineteenth century, that the movement of history leads toward ever greater rational instrumentality. Instead of going over the causes of the decline of evolutionism, it is more important to insist upon the dangers inherent in that which seems to have taken its place, namely *historicism*. The difference between the two lies in the following: evolutionism, which is of German origin, insists upon the particular character of the itinerary taken by every collective actor, guided by a will and oriented by a given culture and history. Today, when history is replete with the conflictual multiplicity of models of development, historicism prevails whereas evolutionism is in full regression. Our societies, which thought that they spoke in the name of universal values, have been reminded, and often quite brutally, that they had been colonialist societies, that they still are the centers of imperialism, and that they still make the weight of their economic and military power felt over a large part of the globe. The cultural crisis of the sixties also laid to rest the illusion of a linear evolution leading toward ever greater instrumentality, role separation, and coldness in social life. The danger of historicism is that it locks each society up into its particularity, that is, that it makes the societies vanish behind the States, the social systems behind the politics, and more simply the practices behind the discourses.

This is why the most important, and the most practical, task of sociology today is to define the relations between the analysis of social systems and the analysis of historical transformations, between synchronic and diachronic analyses. This presupposes, of course, that one acknowledges their separateness. The simplest way of asserting it is to recognize that there obtains no historical change, no passage from one type of society to another, from one field of historicity to another, that is purely endogenous. All social change is, to a greater or lesser extent, *exogenous*. This makes quite obsolete the idea propounded by the Second International that a type of society could develop only when the preceding type had exhausted all of its particularities. Even the most dominant societies do not change as a result of the simple accumulation of their techniques, their riches, and their exchanges. They are just as exposed as dependent and colonized societies to external causes of change and, more precisely, to nonsocial factors, factors of military and economic competition. War is more than ever an important factor of societal change. In the past, a military conquest frequently superimposed a State order upon a local economic life which did not undergo any basic change as a result. In other cases, conquest set a market or industrial economy on top of an agrarian one. But today the linkage between scientific and technological research, large economic investments, and military strategies is so tight that it is impossible to speak of the internal passage from an industrial economy to a postindustrial one. The creation of modern techniques may still be part of the reserved space of the State and of the armed forces in the Soviet Union, but such is not the case in the United States and in the large Western countries, where military and strategic options have much more widespread impact on investments and on the general organization of production. The more ''modern'' the societies are, the more fragile they turn out to be, the more they depend upon changes that take place in their environment. This old idea, by means of which the more rapid economic progress of maritime societies has been explained, is more useful than ever. One can conceive of societies closed upon themselves reducing as far as possible the pressures of the economic and political environment. Such societies can make profound changes in their social organization — witness China and even more so Cambodia — but they are not moved to transform their production capabilities. Nevertheless, it is the conjunction of military danger, on one side, and the will to play an international role, on the other, that impel China to develop modern forms of production today. Similarly, in the nineteenth century, it was the threat posed by the American and Russian fleets that ushered the Meiji revolution in Japan and the speeded up industrialization of its economy.

An analysis of the society as a set of action systems must have as its necessary counterpart the acknowledgment of the exogenous nature of change. This in turn must lead to a more general idea. The chief actors of societal change cannot be the same as those who are at the center of the workings of a society. First, it is not possible to speak of the transformation of industrial society when one speaks of its mode of functioning. Industrial society is a social system; what changes is England or Japan, that is, a political and territorial society, defined geographically and historically. The identity of this national society is represented by a State, not by a ruling class. The State is the agent that represents a society in its intersocial relations; it is, by the same token, the expression of a society as actor of its own history. It establishes the relationship of the present with the past and with the future, as well as the relation of the inside with the outside. There is no State without the right to wage war or peace. Therefore there isn't any State that does not have the capability to commit the life and future of a society. Nor is there any that is not the guarantor of the social order, that is, of the whole of the mechanisms of reproduction. The State is located on the *axis of order and change,* and not that of action and crisis. This is easier to accept if one distinguishes clearly between State and *political system.*

Here too we must put an end to the ethnocentrism inherent in the central capitalist societies within which the State, at least within their boundaries, seems to be frequently confused with the government, if not even with the elected representatives of the people. The political system is a system for the representation of social interests. It is therefore subordinated to class relations, at the same time possessing an autonomy that derives primarily from the complexity of any national society, any social formation. In liberal societies this autonomy is large, and the importance of the political system is so considerable that the State seems to almost disappear. It is indeed in the England of Marx's day that the State withered away the most; but one cannot forget, even in that case, that this State was alive indeed when it was a question of developing and preserving the Empire and of confronting the competition of other industrial nations. Nothing could be farther from the truth and more superficial than the assertion of the identity of the State and of the ruling class. That the ruling class, through the domination that it exerts more or less powerfully over the political system, has a great influence on the State, no one has ever forgotten; but the most important and the most constant historical phenomenon is *the distance that separates the State from the ruling class.* The economic development of Italy, Germany, and Japan was made possible far more as a result of State initiatives than by the action of national bourgeoisies. And, as soon as one leaves the centers of capitalist industrialization, the role of the State in historical transformations is so manifestly dominant that it seems absurd to make it the servant of a ruling class that generally does not even exist or that is slated for liquidation by the State. Whether in Algeria or in Brazil, Mexico or Singapore, Vietnam or the Congo, Iraq or Poland, it is the State that directs the industrialization and the transformation of the society.

It is vain to seek to reduce this State power to a class reality, by speaking, for example, of a State bourgeoisie. The two words do not belong to the same vocabulary, and their coupling does no more than occult a problem that must be treated directly. To be sure, the State is no stranger to the interests and power relations that dominate civil society; but this banal observation does not justify in the least the confusion between two orders of problems, those of the workings of societies and those of their transformation. This distinction becomes clear only if one goes beyond the opposition of State to civil society to oppose more generally the *mode of production* of a society to its *mode of development*. This leads in turn to a reexamination of the most commonly accepted ideas.

I have already said that classes and class relations are located in a mode of production, or, more precisely, in a type of historicity and especially a type of investment. These are class relations that are specific to industrial society, for example, and, on this score, I stressed the fact that these class relations were the same in a capitalist society as in a socialist one, which leads me to say that what we call *capitalism and socialism are neither modes of production nor class relations but modes of industrialization*. Capitalism is the creation of a market, industrial or postindustrial society by a *national bourgeoisie;* one can speak of *dependent* capitalism when economic transformation is directed by a *foreign bourgeoisie* or, more exactly, by a capitalist system the center of which lies outside the concerned country. We have frequently called *socialist* the countries in which the transformation was conducted by a *national State* that had broken with dependent participation in the global capitalist system. I underscore the following assertion: capitalism is not a mode of production, and furthermore, that capitalism does not define class relations. It is a regime, a mode of development, a social form of economic development and, in particular, of industrialization. The ownership of the means of production is one thing; the social relations of production, another. Capitalist accumulation and socialist—that is, State—accumulation take extremely different forms, but their class signification is the same inasmuch as they create industrial societies in both cases, that is, production ensembles in which the workers are subordinated to a so-called rationalized organization of labor under the direction of the holders of capital. The separation of these two realms condemns the ideological discourse that refers to a national society by defining it on every occasion as either socialist or capitalist. The fact that assembly-line workers are subjected to exhausting production rhythms and to output-based systems of reward has nothing to do with capitalism, but it is one of the most important problems of industrial society. On the other hand, one does not have the right to denounce some inconveniences or some scandals of highly industrialized and urbanized societies by laying the blame for them at the door-steps either of capitalism or of socialism.

When one speaks today, within an industrialized capitalist society, of the passage to socialism, what does one mean? The phrase has several meanings. The most concrete is the one that asserts the necessity of reinforcing the intervention of the State within the economic sphere, to develop the public sector at the expense of the private, because the latter is unable to face the deep transformations and investments that are required by a threatening international environment or by important technological innovations. A second meaning, which bears no relation to the first, insists on the necessity of reinforcing the influence or the power of the workers vis-à-vis their employers, be they private or public, within the work environment and in the whole of social life, As for expressions like "transition to socialism" that imply that socialism is a historical stage that comes after capitalism, they are simply devoid of meaning. One need recall one more time that if many industrial capitalist societies have become to some degree socialist, to the extent at least that the intervention of the State increased within them, no capitalist society has turned socialist by itself, in the sense that one means that the Soviet Union or China are socialist. Political life in countries such as France makes the greatest use of completely empty phrases which those who use them take great pains not to define. We hear that such and such a party does not mean to effect a passage to socialism but will be content to set up an advanced democracy. But this advance is itself conceived of as a first step toward socialism, that is, toward State ownership of the means of production. One could not satisfy those who use such phrases if one told them that they are perfectly acceptable provided that they do not imply any transformation in the conditions of the workers nor any change in class relations. It is therefore simpler to give up such slogans, which had a meaning only at a time when an evolutionist conception of history prevailed naturally, as if social regimes followed each other in the majestic parade of history.

We cannot remain content, however, with the simple separation of the study of the system from that of development. Everyone knows the two studies cannot entirely be isolated one from the other; if they intersect, we must learn how to locate their meeting point, which happens to be the central area of sociological analysis. This must be taken literally. The central problem of sociological analysis is indeed that of the relations between the diachronic and the synchronic, between the State and the ruling class. A great many social thinkers have, for a very long time, been quite aware of the central position occupied by this question in any conception of society. One could add another formulation to the ones already used: what is the relation between class movements and national movements? Class movements have a central place in the workings of society, whereas national movements are the most important collective movements as far as historical change is concerned since the latter is always dominated by the figure of the State. This issue is more familiar to historians than to sociologists; it appeared for the first time in dazzling fashion within Austro-Marxist thought and has gained in importance as so-called socialist revolutions or transformations occurred more frequently in regions under the domination of autocratic national States or colonizing foreign States.

Synchronic and diachronic analyses do not simply intersect; their relation is inscribed in the analysis of the social system and especially in that of class relations. It is well known that the latter have two aspects: relations of production between a ruling class and a laboring and protesting class, on the one hand, and relations of reproduction between a dominant and a dominated class, on the other. There are the antagonistic classes that vie for the control of historicity, and the more acute their conflict, the more it develops the forces of production and of change in relation to crisis factors and to the forces of reproduction. When, however, a dominant class is primarily engaged in a defense of its privileges, and a popular class defends its traditional way of life, neither needs to refer to historicity and they both seek then the State as the battleground for the conflict that opposes them, or as an ally against their opponent. *The distance between the ruling class and the State is determined by the distance between the relations of production and the relations of reproduction.* Wherever, and for the most diverse reasons, the ruling class is actually a dominant class, it must rely upon the State to bring about respect for the order that favors it and to repress the attempts to transform this order. The popular classes, for their part, must then attack the State as chief protector of a class that, without the support of its arms and its laws, would be incapable of defending itself. In those places where the State is nothing but the corrupt and artificially preserved agent of a colonizing State, social struggle can even concentrate itself in areas of an armed struggle against the State. This was true of the Cuban guerrilla warfare against Batista; it still is true case of the guerrilla war in El Salvador; and if guerrilla movements failed in Venezuela, Peru, and even in Bolivia, it was because the State in these countries by no means resembled the one brought down by Fidel Castro or that of Somoza. In France it is because industrialization has been conducted more often by the State than by the bourgeoisie and because the latter has been quite busy defending its privileges and putting together a block of oligarchic interests, that the action of the labor movement has been often subordinated to the action of the Communist party against the State. On the other hand, in England at the end of the nineteenth century and in the early twentieth century, and in the United States since the creation of the American Federation of Labor, action has been almost completely dissociated from any action against the State and, on the contrary, strongly associated with the action of political parties seeking institutional transformations.

The closer one gets to the center of capitalist economy, the more civil society appears to dominate the State to the point that the latter can appear to be no more than the agent of the ruling class. But the farther one goes from the central countries, the more one encounters different situations, whose effects, however, are the same at the general level of analysis we are considering here. On one side, dependent or colonized countries, which are subordinated to external economic initiatives, are largely dominated by political struggles against oligarchies. On the other, the countries that were neither colonized nor carried away in the first movement of industrialization are the ones in which the State intervenes as the defender of a social order in the service of former dominant classes that no longer play a leading or innovative economic role. In all these instances, political action supplants social struggle.

It is in synchronic analysis itself that the explanation of its relations with diachronic analysis is thus to be found, and this fact grants it a decisive privilege. But, as we have just seen, it is also in the domination exerted by the State, be it autocratic and conservative or bent on conquest in the service of dynamic capitalism, that resides the explanation for the disjunction between ruling class and dominant class, and for the superiority of the latter. Nothing marks more clearly the bond between these two great orders of analysis than the notion of *revolution.* By definition, this notion associates a popular social movement, or a nonruling class, with a political action of overturning the State. These two elements cannot be conflated. In the French Revolution, peasants and artisans rise against landowners and merchants while, at the same time, the bourgeoisie overturns privileges and royal power. The history of the French revolution is made up of the changing relations between this social movement and this political action, Robespierre having positioned himself at the central point of the revolution owing to the fact that he wanted to combine both these meanings: he was both the man of the Terror and that of the maximal program. His fall bears witness to the fragility of this compromise, and it was followed by the triumph of the bourgeoisie. The character of Lenin is even more important because he pushed this ambiguity even farther. Above all, he was a party man and a protagonist in the struggle against the existing State and the creation of a new one, but he was also, especially at the decisive moment when he wrote *The State and the Revolution* and *The April Theses,* the man of the popular and labor movements and of the social revolution. During his last years of rule, though he privileged almost entirely the construction of the State and of the party, the will to remain the interpreter of a social movement could be felt within him. Following his death, the tendency that his most important acts had already set into motion was accentuated, and the party-state gobbled up the social movement with which he had accomplished the revolution. We call Stalinism this State that devours its father, but the same central phenomenon can be found in almost all Communist regimes. That is the difference between Communist totalitarianism and Fascist totalitarianism, with the latter destroying its social opponents rather than the forces that brought it to power.

Marxist thought, considered as a whole, is the doctrine that has interpreted the ideology of the labor movement. When the latter was the principal social movement, Marxist thought was vigorous, independent, critical, and it had to wage hard battles against bourgeois ideologies to gain recognition. Then Marxist thought stopped being the autonomous expression of a social movement in order to become primarily the doctrine of Communist parties, and, to a lesser extent, that of socialist parties, though the latter cared little, if truth be told, about doctrine elaboration, especially after World War I and even less after World War II. The association of Marxist thought with Communist parties on a global scale, and even in Western Europe, has had as a consequence an almost complete withering away of Marxist reflection.

This example, drawn from the history of ideas, shows the failure of all attempts to unify the analysis of systems with that of historical transformations. Sociological analysis must recognize the separation of these two axes of analysis, before associating itself with the work of historians in order to understand the practical forms of their combination.

Chapter 9
The Method of Action Sociology: Sociological Intervention

The choice of method does not rest upon technical considerations alone. Every method corresponds to an approach, to a representation of social reality, and therefore to the researcher's option of privileging a given type of behavior. Anthropologists or sociologists whose interest in nature and in the way social and cultural norms function in a given collectivity runs more to issues of order than to problems of change must adopt the observer's position. They will seek to locate the objective signs of these representations, beliefs, myths, which they will analyze from the outside; that is, by searching for the principles that preside over sets of rules and even over the mental structures involved in the elaboration of these myths and beliefs.

Sociologists who are interested in the social determination of behavior, especially in the forms and levels of social participation, must turn to extensive survey-taking. They seek to show the correspondence between status and role, or the determinant role of social position or of mobility along the social scale upon behavior. This is indeed the most classical approach of modern sociology. Advances in statistical methods have renewed it, and the success of Parsonian functionalism in the fifties gave it such an importance that, for a while, it was possible to believe that it stood for all of sociology. Those who are primarily interested in decision-making, transformations, power-and influence relations have never been satisfied with this representation of society, however, nor with surveys. They have always preferred to study how decisions were made, how organizations were changing, and this led them to develop case studies that sought to reconstruct the complex and hidden history of decision-making behind the facade of seamless appearances.

Finally, those who are interested in what one could somewhat broadly call social movements have, until now, relied upon a method that is more directly historical. As they inquired into the nature of the social and political forces capable of transforming a society and of bringing about historical events, they generally concluded that one should examine the most momentous events, those in the course of which the old social order appears to dissolve and a new one comes into being. Georges Gurvitch, in particular, who was led to sociology by the experience of the Russian Revolution, defended the idea that one should look into the volcanoes of history, as if revolutions had a purifying value and made possible a contact with what is essential. If today, however, there is no reason to cast doubt upon the usefulness of ethnographic observation or survey-taking or studies of decision-making, the same cannot be said about the philosophy of history implicated in the last approach, with its concentration on great events and on revolutions in particular. We no longer put much stock in this image of a social order tearing itself asunder in order to release the creative forces of history. The experience of the twentieth century has taught us to be more prudent. Great events and revolutions are no simpler than periods of calm. One could even think that the revolutionary movement is the one in which social forces are least visible, most covered over by the problems of the State, occurring at a time when social mechanisms are most completely replaced by the dictatorship of the gun or that of the word. And this to such an extent that times of revolutions, which continue to be major objects of reflection for historians, are probably the least favorable moments for a reflection on historical action, as if in the very instant when human beings may indeed be making their history, they are in a particularly poor position to understand the history they are making and even inclined to do the opposite of what they think they are doing.

Sociologists interested in the study of historical action find themselves thus practically devoid of method. They cannot hold on to a historical analysis that would elicit its own meaning from itself, as the historians and sociologists of the nineteenth century thought, from Michelet to Weber. The former, followed in this by many Central European historians, saw the birth of the nation at the heart of modern history; the latter saw in it the stages of a disillusionment of the world, of secularization and rationalization. These evolutionist and unilinear visions seem somewhat lacking today. They explain neither regresses into barbarism nor the multiplicity of ways of developing. It would appear, then, that there is no method for studying the way in which a society produces its cultural models, its social relations, and its practices. Sociological intervention is the method that attempts to fill this void. It wants to be in the service of the study of the production of society, just as the survey is in the service of the study of the forms and levels of social participation.

Principles

1. The main problem is that the realm of the most basic social relations and of their cultural stakes is not available for unmediated observation. How does one go from the study of norm response behavior to that of behavior that brings the norms into question? Already in an altogether different context, Marx was trying to recover class relations behind the categories of economic praxis. Similarly, many people looked behind workers' attitudes, that is, behind their responses to work and life situations, for the manifestation of a workers' consciousness and in particular a class consciousness. The fact that within daily experience there is a constant calling into question of one's individual situation was the first major finding of industrial sociology, thanks to the classical studies of Roethlisberger at Western Electric.[1] Studying slowdowns in the Bank Wiring shop, these first industrial sociologists showed that workers' behavior, far from being definable in terms of adaptability or rationality, had to be understood as the concrete expression of a struggle for the control of the machines and of the output. All the studies on workers' behavior in the face of various forms of rewards have constantly reinforced the conclusions of this pioneering research. This example leads us into a direction completely opposed to that of the study of "great historical events." It is by concentrating our attention upon the actors themselves as we apprehend them under the conditions of their concrete existence that we will come closest to the mechanisms by means of which we can get a glimpse, beyond behavior related to social consumption, of behavior engaged in the conflictual production of the society.

2. But we must go beyond observation. We must create in a quasi-experimental way places in which the weight of daily situations will be lightened as much as possible, thus allowing the actors to express as strongly as possible their opposition and challenge to this situation, their objectives and the consciousness they have of the conflicts they are engaged in to accomplish these objectives. The study of historical action requires the apparent paradox of a distance from broad frescoes and extensive opinion surveys and instead the practice of intensive studies of restricted groups, researched at length and in depth.

3. Let us go even further. The passage from consumption to production of society does not occur spontaneously, even under the favorable conditions set up by the researchers. The latter must intervene directly. It is only through them that actors can rise from one level of social reality to another and go from response and adaptation behavior to behavior of project elaboration and conflict. It is only if the researchers intervene actively and personally to draw the actors toward the most basic relations in which they are engaged that the latter will be able to stop defining themselves only by responding to the established order.

Procedures

Let us return to the apparent paradox of studying historical actors, and in particular class actors and their social movements, through small groups. Not that this constitutes a genuine contradiction. The social actors themselves are used to seeing small-scale groups constitute the base units of their movement: political cells, union shops, small religious communities, local associations, all groups that are bearers of high historical significance. The problem is that, for complex reasons, interest in small groups has been associated in the social sciences with the reduction of social relations to interpersonal relations — an unwarranted step. To remain within the specific realm of social psychology, how could one forget that Lewin was first concerned with Nazism, that Moreno wanted to recover the spirit of the Russian Revolution, and that Serge Moscovici has just shown how the study of active minorities, as conducted by a social psychologist, could have broad political signification?[2] W. Doise, in his recent thesis,[3] insists on the necessity to strengthen this sociological orientation in the study of groups. What matters here is not the size of the group studied but the fact that there be constituted *intervention groups* placed in an artificial situation such that their members see themselves, in this situation more so than in their ordinary existence, as the producers of their history, their stories, and as the transformers of their situations.

The starting point of sociological intervention is the constitution of such groups, composed of actors, in the sociological sense, or, more precisely, of activists who never have to leave the field of their action but who commit themselves, as activists, to a work of analysis. There should be no contradiction between the role of activist and the role of analyst since the analysis is directed at uncovering the deepest meaning of the action. But in practice the formation of such groups encounters great difficulties. All actors seek to retain mastery over their own meaning; their ideology proves resistant to analysis. We have experienced the especially strong resistance not of the activists themselves but of the "organic" intellectuals, who purport to speak in their name and to be the producers of their ideology. In addition, the formation of such groups presupposes an attitude of the researcher that cannot be one of neutrality. To establish the necessary relation between actors and analysts, the latter must be perceived as putting themselves in the service of neither the actors nor their ideology but that of their possible meaning. Whoever the actors may be, the researcher must look for the highest possible signification of their action, their role as producers of history.

If one were to interrogate the groups about their opinions and their attitudes, if one were to encourage them to articulate their ideology, one would have moved away from the desired goal; one would merely reinforce the group's responses to a given situation. One must therefore select an altogether opposite research procedure: no sooner are the groups formed than they are brought to face interlocutors who are their social partners—friends or foes—in real life. One replaces thus the expression of an ideology by the experience of a social relation. The selection of the interlocutors is made, as far as it is possible, by the groups themselves. The researchers limit themselves to orienting the exchange of views between actors and interlocutors. Their chief task is to prevent the two parties from avoiding discussion or from placing artificial limits upon it. It is equally important that the greatest possible variety be evident in the group. Indeed each group is constituted in such a way that the principal components of the struggle or of the concerned action are present within it. The meeting with interlocutors should be replaced in the future with a more cumbersome procedure since one should study simultaneously actors engaged in a social relation, employers and wage earners, for example, as we did in our study on the labor movement, on colonizers and colonized, State rulers and dissidents, and so on.

Following the meetings with the interlocutors, the researchers serve as moderators of "closed" sessions in which the groups comment upon the encounters that have taken place and thus begin the analysis of their action.

Researchers are indeed less interested in the behavior of the actors than in their self-analysis. It is inconceivable to separate the role of consciousness from the role itself, or, in particular, class from class consciousness. Even when this class consciousness is mixed up with the consciousness of other roles or covered up by the latter and, especially, deformed into an ideology, it is nonetheless present. The first goal of researchers is, then, to develop the consciousness of the actor. When they begin to meet, groups act as *sample groups,* that is, their discussions reproduce the debates that develop in the struggle or in the collective action. These sample groups must be transformed into *figural groups* through a *reversal* which requires that one distance oneself from praxis and produce general interpretations of the praxis in the process. This passage can take place spontaneously or at the initiative of researchers. It leads to what one could call ideological analysis, since this analysis remains tied to action at the same time that it seeks to understand it.

Conversion is the passage from this ideological analysis to an analysis that seeks to identify the social movement present in the action. Researchers alone can effect this passage.It is up to them to present to the group the image of the social movement that gives the action its highest meaning. Researchers, at this stage, no longer seek to interpret the nature of a praxis by the uncovering of its "spirit"; rather they draw both the praxis and its interpretation to the highest level. They never place themselves at any other level than that of social movements. Their role is to bring into view the forms and force under which society-producing behavior is present in behavior that may be analyzed or perceived at other levels of social life. Such a conversion necessarily takes a dramatic form since it is a matter of extracting a signification from a praxis and of bringing about the recognition that it is this signification that gives its meaning to the other aspects of the action. What is essential here is to know how the group behaves with respect to this hypothesis. Will the hypothesis elicit clear and stable reactions? Does it make the relations among the group members more intelligible? Does it allow them to reinterpret their past action as well as the history of the group? Finally, does the hypothesis allow the group to elaborate an action program and to anticipate the responses it may elicit? All the moments of the intervention that follow the conversion must remain under the latter's sway; the conversion itself can be considered as having been truly effected only at the end of the research. It is not enough, however, to establish the validity of the hypothesis in the groups in which it has been presented. It is desirable to submit the hypothesis to other groups. This represents an important part of what is called *permanent sociology*, which is the set of research operations that follow conversion. New groups are formed to apply the hypotheses to new situations and to see if these hypotheses help them to better analyze their action and the reactions it elicits.

Problems

The scope of the conclusions to be drawn from an intervention has some limitations. By choosing an intensive, as opposed to an extensive, method one accepts certain inconveniences, the most severe of which is the interdiction to make historical predictions—something one can do with extensive studies and which is their strong point.

Sociological intervention in a collective action does not permit an evaluation of the chances this action has of acquiring some historical importance. One could even imagine that an intervention would show the virtual importance of an action and yet lead to thinking that this action will not have any historical importance. The first of the studies we conducted took the 1976 student strike in France as its object; the strike was a failure, and we showed that it was in fact the end of the student New Left in France. It was by showing the conditions under which the student struggle could have become a social movement that we were best able to bring out the failure of this strike, a strike with altogether different objectives and an ideology quite at variance with those that could have animated a social movement. In revealing the nature of a possible social movement, we showed that the strike was moving away from that possibility, but at no point were we in a position to demonstrate that its failure was inevitable.

Similarly, our study of the antinuclear movement came to the conclusion that there was an antitechnocratic social movement in these struggles, but, equally, that the scope of this signification upon the practices of antinuclear activists was quite limited. Ultimately it allowed a forecast that this movement would seek a practice halfway between antinuclear feelings and an antinuclear movement by organizing itself into a political current. But we could not tell what the chances and the importance of this political movement would be. The goal of sociological intervention is not the prediction of events but the analysis of the mechanism through which collective action and, at a higher level, social movements, are formed.

The most difficult problem concerns the role of the investigators. It is necessarily a double role since the researchers must elicit and follow the self-analysis of the actors while drawing the group toward conversion by taking the initiative of presenting it with a certain image of itself. Investigators must therefore keep the distance between knowing and doing as far as the group is concerned but, at the same time, remain close to the actors, their ideologies, and their concrete objectives. This requires that the research roles be divided among two persons. I call *interpreter* the investigator who remains close to the self-analysis of the group, who "pushes" the group forward, and who strives to avoid any rupture between its experience of real struggle and its activity in the framework of the intervention. I call *analyst* the one who generally adopts the viewpoint of the analysis and who seeks to elaborate hypotheses from the behavior of the group during the first phase of the intervention. This differentiation between the two functions is the more pronounced as the action is the more distant from the social movement that it may be bearing. If the distance were unbridgeable, there could be no communication between the two researchers, and the crisis that would then arise in the research team would be a good indication of the absence of a social movement in the struggle. Conversely, if the action is heavily laden with a social movement, the two researchers can work side by side and the interpreter can play a direct and important role in the conversion. In any case, the main danger for the researchers is probably not to keep enough distance from the group and to identify too closely with it. This can be explained by ideological causes but also by other, more concrete, ones. The individual researcher depends upon the group for the success of the research; she needs therefore to be accepted by it and thinks that the way to do it is by reducing the distance that separates them, by showing her loyalty to the group and its struggle, going as far perhaps as identifying with it and sometimes by seeking to become its leader. A strong identification of the researcher with the group can create the illusion that the group is capable of carrying its self-analysis quite far. But it leads to the impossibility of effecting a conversion since it abolishes the distance between the researcher and the group, whereas conversion presupposes as large a distance as possible and a considerable effort by the researcher to "pull" the group toward the highest meaning of its action, of which it becomes the bearer.

What I have stated so far will give rise to the objection that is constantly raised against sociological intervention: the latter has no demonstrative value because its very procedures supposedly ensure it of success, but an artificial one. Intervention would then be a sort of suggestiveness, the more easily carried out as the researcher projects a very gratifying image of her practice and has taken on a leadership position. It would then be easy for the researcher to assert that a social movement is present in any struggle whatsoever.

This objection calls for several rejoinders. First, conversion is not judged by the assent of the group to the hypothesis presented by the researcher at a given moment. What validates the hypothesis is the capacity of the group to reinterpret and to orient its past, present, and future experience as a function of the presented hypotheses. One must recall in addition that the research protocol presupposes the intervention of several investigators into several groups and in several stages frequently separated by several months. To these general arguments, one must add a concrete experience with much more weight. During the course of a study on the Occitan movement in France, I elaborated and introduced a hypothesis that was rejected by the two groups; we then formulated another hypothesis that another investigator, François Dubet, introduced to the groups and which was rejected in turn. The greatest part of the subsequent phases of the research was devoted to the analysis and the interpretation of this double failure. It is therefore demonstrated by experience that a hypothesis can be rejected by the groups concerned even when the relations between investigators and groups are excellent and no explanation of the so-called psychosociological order can be invoked. It must be added that such a failure is not one of method; on the contrary, it proves that some groups can effect their "conversion," that is, place themselves in the perspective of a possible social movement but, at the same time, recognize that this movement cannot be embodied in their action and that the latter cannot attain such lofty objectives. Conversion does not consist in recognizing the highest possible conflicts in all actual claims but in situating the latter in relation to that level of social action.

Another objection that is sometimes raised is that we do not take into account specifically psychosociological phenomena that occur in the groups. Actually, when one looks at groups, one can be interested in different phenomena. Those whose methods draw upon psychoanalysis are particularly interested in the nature of the social bond or may be trying to combat forms of military or religious authority that arise in groups. Yet others may be interested in the ways in which a group will behave in a given situation or adapt to change and make decisions. I see no need to oppose the internal functioning of the group to the problems of the struggle in which its members are engaged, since a considerable part of the events that occur within the group, and of the relations that form between its members, must be interpreted in the light of our hypotheses, which are properly sociological. Indeed it is in the change of one of the members of the group—for example, a loss of leadership or the rejection by the group of one of its members—that one often finds the most direct signs of the nature of the relations between a social practice and its raison d'être.

Field of Application

An essential question is whether sociological intervention has as its sole field of application what current language calls social movements, and this only in advanced industrial societies. An essential part of the work of those who will be convinced of the interest of this method must be the study of the conditions and forms under which it can be applied to other social fields and to other social situations.

First, it is indispensable that the method not limit itself to oppositional or popular movements. It is essential to show that one can study in the same way the behavior of ruling milieux. One of our top objectives should be the setting up of sociological intervention upon the ruling class, especially with the leaders of large organizations, private or public, whether industrial of not. Naturally it would be desirable to have such interventions conducted in several industrial countries with different cultural traditions, for example, in selected countries in Europe and North America, and in Japan. More generally, it is essential that interventions carried out on social struggles be completed by analogous research conducted in other countries, especially in dependent or formerly colonized countries, in which peasant or urban movements play an important role.

But it is also urgent to go farther away from the realm proper to social movements, to come down from this high level to the study of political and organizational behavior, then to that of the behavior of order, crisis, and change, which correspond to the other "areas" of sociological analysis and which may carry within them the deformed presence of behaviors of historicity and of social movements. For instance, in countries in which industrialization was directed by authoritarian regimes, social relations are covered over by relation of order and by state domination.

Finally, one must even seek to remove oneself from social movements. Behavior of individual deviance or even of madness can be analyzed, in part at least, as forms of the individualized expression of an impossible social movement, a deprivation of historical action. The method of sociological intervention will have to be adapted to this extreme dissociation of the meaning of an action from its form of social appearances.

Everything in this discussion has rested on a certain confidence that it is possible for social movements to appear. But one should grant equal importance to what one could call *social antimovements,* that is, to everything that appeals in a defensive way to a community and to its consensus against an external enemy. What under some conditions can blossom into a social movement can, under others, close up into an antimovement. The workers' movement has sometimes closed upon itself into an authoritarian group that rejected minorities. Today, on a global scale, movements of community defense are growing in importance, with their opposition to authoritarian and brutal industrialization which appears to be directed from the outside.

Should one draw the conclusion from these brief indications that step by step the method of sociological intervention means to impose itself on the whole of sociology? Yes and no. It is impossible indeed to decide a priori that a given type of social behavior has no relation to the field of historicity and to the social movements it is animated by. But it would be as big an error to believe that one could reduce all social behavior to behavior of the highest level. That is why one must oppose two orders of behavior: behavior of action and behavior of order. There is no modern society without order, without State, without war. This immense realm faces the social world, which is that of social relations and of their cultural stakes. One wonders with some anxiety whether the open space of civil society, which has slowly been extended in the West over the past centuries, is not going to be reclaimed again by the jungle of the State. One of the chief tasks of sociology is to defend foot by foot this clearing and the cultures that human collectivities developed in it. The method of sociological intervention works to such a defense. To be sure, it has cognitve aims, but it also seeks to raise the level of action so that actual action comes ever closer to the maximal possible action. It seeks to help human beings make their history, at a time when, upon the ruins of destroyed and betrayed illusions, the confidence in societies' capacity to produce themselves is diminished. There is no contradiction in saying that sociological intervention has a heuristic value and in recognizing that it is also the sign of a desire to rekindle the awareness of possible action, and thus it contributes to defend and to reinforce the chances of democracy.

PART III

Questioning
The
Present

Chapter 10
The Birth of Programmed Society

We are leaving the shores of industrial society, but whither? Are we drifting away? Are we sailing to Cythera or are we going to land in hyperindustrial society? Are we in the midst of a decadence, or, after several centuries of growth, are we coming back to societies more preoccupied with equilibrium,, not unlike our rural societies of yore? Or are we perhaps on our way to a society capable of exerting a higher level of intervention upon itself than industrial society, one we could call, provisionally, postindustrial society?

The risk of decadence is no doubt present. Used to abundance, our societies are concerned with guarantees and pleasure and allow themselves to be dragged into the future backward. Such views are more seductive than convincing, however, and provide little understanding of present-day problems. The important question remains: are we going through a new period of growth or through a return to equilibrium? Is this the threshold of postindustrial society or a passage into a posthistorical society? the end of a stage of development or the end of development itself? We have recently gone through a strong countercultural movement which cast doubt directly on the values of industrialization and growth and sought equilibrium and identity in all of their forms. It could not be more than a brief transitional phase between the rejection of the values of industrial society and the realization of the transformation of the economic order. The exhaustion of industrial society in the countries where it had developed the most foretells the difficult but necessary passage to a new type of society, one more active and more mobile, and even more dangerous, than the one we are leaving.

A Level of Historicity

The definition, given earlier in these pages, of industrial society as the society in which investment is used primarily to transform the organization of labor, requires that we conceive of a postindustrial society that propels historicity, primarily through investment, to a level not reached by industrial society, that of the ends of production. The organization of labor reached only the manufacturing level and thus the relations of workers among themselves. This was an intervention that eventually rose to the level of management, that is, to the whole of production, first by innovation, the capacity to invent products on the basis of scientific and technological investments, then by management in the strict sense of the term, that is, by the capacity to make complex organizations and decision-making systems. The passage to postindustrial society takes place when investment results in the production of symbolic goods that modify values, needs, representations, far more than in the production of material goods or even of "services." Industrial society had transformed the means of production; postindustrial society changes the ends of production, that is, culture.

To be sure, levels of historicity do not admit of such simple succession. A country that reaches a certain level of historicity continues to exploit the lower levels, which are characteristic of earlier societies. An industrial country does not give up the benefits acquired through commerce; a postindustrial society does not give up the organization of labor. But the specificity of a particular society lies in its recognition of the greater importance of a certain type of investment and the disposition to arbitrate in its favor when it conflicts with another type, one characteristic of an earlier form of society. Thus a postindustrial society cannot be defined, any more than an industrial one, by a given technology. It is just as superficial to speak of a computer society or of a plutonium society as it is of steam-engine society or an electric motor society. Nothing justifies the granting of such a privilege to a particular technology, whatever its economic importance. The decisive point here is that in postindustrial society all of the economic system is the object of intervention of society upon itself.

That is why we can call it the *programmed society,* because this phrase captures its capacity to create models of management, production, organization, distribution, and consumption, so that such a society appears, at all its functional levels, as the product of an action exercised by the society itself, and not as the outcome of natural laws or cultural specificities.

The Lived Experience of Programmed Society

Let us now change our perspective and place ourselves in the position of those who live this society, who experience it, and who, especially at the industrial level, behave like consumers rather than producers with respect to it. This is where quantitative analyses find their place.

During what Carl Polanyi called *the great transformation*,[1] that is, industrialization, it was possible for sociologists to consider more often the breakup of the forms of earlier social life and the development of the market rather than the organization of labor. The inverse of exchanges within a social whole seemed to many to constitute the most important change, what Karl Deutsch in the United States[2] and Gino Germani in Argentina[3] have named almost simultaneously, the level of "mobilization" of a society. A programmed society is experienced as having a higher degree of mobilization than an industrial one. In the latter, individuals are drawn into oriented systems of collective organization at the level of work; the specificity of postindustrial society lies in the introduction of large centralized management apparatuses in the most diverse realms of social life. That is why it has been possible to speak of the industrialization of so many things: information, consumption, health, scientific research, and even general education. The term is inaccurate but does indicate that there are forming decision-making and management centers capable of providing not only systems of means but objectives of social life, producing health, consumer, and information technologies. This mobilization gives greater opportunities to individuals, but it also risks increasing the manipulatory capacity of an absolute power.

The extraordinary acceleration and multiplication of programmed communications elicits at first very positive attitudes that we must not let the strength of the countercultural protests of recent years occult. To begin with, most of those who participate in this type of society are attracted by the multiplication of information and therefore by the choices offered. It is arbitrary to oppose the concentration of decision-making power and the uniformization of messages or programs. Where such uniformization exists, it is due not to the inherent nature of a programmed society but to something completely different, namely the nature of the system of political and ideological control proper to some countries. One must beware of overly easy or simply elitist critiques of the mass media. Those who, in the past, had a very broad freedom of material or intellectual consumption, have an even greater freedom of choice, as is evidenced by their intense desire to have access to societies and cultures removed from theirs in space and time. And those who were locked in a local framework, under the influence of traditional elites and within the boundaries of popular literature, have access today to a much larger repertory. Programmed society makes individuals, goods, and ideas circulate much more intensely than did earlier societies.

Furthermore, it must be recognized that a society with a very high historicity, a very high self-production capability, reduces considerably the share of reproduction within itself. In fact, it becomes less and less tolerant of anything that is oriented to reproduction, so that less and less behavior and behavioral schemes are reproduced. This translates itself often by what are called liberation movements, the chief meaning of which, whether they are liberal, libertarian, or revolutionary, is the destruction of established situations and ascribed roles, thus propelling all population categories into ever more intense exchanges and communications. The women's liberation movement in particular found its starting point in the general crisis of "ascribed status." This propulsion is as strong and as ambiguous as the one that moved the founders of industrial capitalist society to fight against slavery and against anything that stood in the way of the free disposition of people on the market. This type of action is indeed destructive of barriers, prejudices, and interdicts, but one must not succumb to the seduction of its frequently revolutionary or libertarian language. It is already being observed that the destruction of the earlier separation between private life and public life, and the more equal participation of women in the whole of economic and professional activities, can be largely explained in terms of the interest of a consumer society in need of raising the level of spendable household income and of broadening the field of market consumption.

This ambiguity proceeds from the fact that cultural innovation develops at first in strict conjunction with the formation of new ruling groups, whereas dominated social categories remain culturally on the defensive, holding on to that which gives them their specificity in order to protect themselves against the domination that comes from the outside. Culturally progressive views can be associated with socially conservative ones. This is why women's groups that wish to oppose such conservatism and yet pursue their task of cultural innovation must signify in spectacular or in violent fashion their differentiation from the ruling milieux and their models of behavior. The fact remains, however, that all the behavior I have just evoked is part of a modernizing attitude, one seeking to open society up, and thus it is one more avatar of Enlightenment philosophy.

Conversely, in the social categories that are at some distance from the ruling sphere as well as in large sectors of intellectual life, especially among individuals whose level of education is higher than their economic status, there is expressed the fear of individuals and groups being confined in thicker and thicker networks of signals, rules, and interdictions. There has been talk of a "wired society," of life behind grids, of normalizing pressures. In preindustrial and culturally traditional societies, some rules were maintained and inculcated in very authoritarian ways, but their network was loose and the areas of indeterminacy quite numerous. In a large modern city, it is literally impossible to take one step without receiving some command, without being exposed to advertising or propaganda, without being confronted with social scales in which one can indicate one's level by oneself. This is why there is a search for nonsocial relations, for interpersonal ones, or such a desire to erect communities conceived as a refuge within an increasingly thicker social network. Marginality, considered for so long a failure of integration, becomes thus the hallmark of an opposition, a laboratory in which a new culture and a social counterproject are being elaborated.

A Technical Society

At a more global level of the critique, there appears the idea that a programmed society increases the distance between rulers and ruled. To be sure, we hear the recurrent notion that the new technologies favor greater decentralization. This is a notion that had already been voiced at the end of the nineteenth century when many argued that electricity would work in favor of decentralization as opposed to coal which had brought on more centralization. Actually, the idea that a technology orders society turns out to be false yet again. It is not in the nature of electricity to determine the social mode of its use; the same is true of computer technology. On the other hand, it is certain that the elaboration of information-producing and-managing apparatuses results in most areas in a concentration of power. Such a concentration has been under way for quite some time in the industrial realm; it has advanced even further now, but the concentration of decision-making power has become even more pronounced in areas where it had limited importance until recently. A frequently studied example is that of scientific research and the passage from ''little science'' to ''big science,'' especially as part of the tremendous arms race between the superpowers. One may even think that a programmed society allows, and stimulates, a greater interdependence among the apparatuses of domination. Isn't an almighty central power capable of imposing its will upon an atomized society through the destruction of communities and traditions, favored by uprooting, modernization, and the acceleration of change?

Beyond these attitudes, both positive and negative, what matters is to return to the question raised earlier of the relations between technology and society. Are we now in a technical society? Must we expect social progress to come from technological advances, with a rise in living standards and an increase in the number of choices? Or must we, on the contrary, acknowledge that some techniques pose a direct threat to us? These questions are indeed new, and the definition we gave earlier of a programmed society does not allow us to abide by the answers provided by nineteenth-century thought, namely that science and technology by themselves have positive effects but they can be given negative ones by their mode of social use. It would then suffice to replace one form of management by another, an oligarchy by a democracy, to transform the forces of death into forces of life, springs of power into fountains of welfare. This kind of distinction between forces of production and social relations of production is today largely artificial. It could work in an industrial society in which social power did not intervene at the level of production itself, but only at the level of the organization of labor. Today, the choices are much more radical, and the specificity of ruling forces lies in their identification with the management of information systems. This simple observation does not lead, however, to the conclusion that our society is directly determined by the techniques it uses.

Quite to the contrary! The time has come to reverse the traditional reasoning. When antinuclear militants say that nuclear industry produces an authoritarian and centralized society or that the civilization of plutonium is a police state whereas a solar society would be a democratic and decentralized one, they are reasoning backward. In point of fact, it is the might of the great decision-making apparatuses that imposes a certain kind of energy policy. In France it is the power of the State electric monopoly and of the Atomic Energy Commission that accounts for the fact that in 1973-74, in the absence of any real political debate, an all-nuclear policy was adopted, as the logical follow-up to the all-electric policy imposed a few years earlier by Electricité de France for commercial considerations.

Technological choices are first and foremost political ones, and their effects convey the state of relations among social forces. The idea is not entirely new: for more than thirty years, industrial psychosociologists have been insisting upon the fact that the effects of technological changes were less dependent upon the necessary consequences of these changes than upon the social mode of the introduction of these changes. Studies on the changes brought about in administrative work by new data-processing methods show how difficult it is to identify the specific consequences of such technical change. The extreme variety of opinions and of observed situations points to the fact that it is impossible to isolate a primary cause of technological origin as the determining factor of all programmed society. The main reason is that social power, being directly located at the level of production, determines and directs the uses of technology: it is not the television set that decides on the programming. In fact it is in the societies farthest removed from programmed society, and even from industrial society, that one could speak accurately of technological determinism insofar as the society's intervention upon itself has little to do with technology or production in such societies but much more, as we saw earlier, with distribution and consumption. In traditional Brazil, for instance, one could well speak of a wood civilization, a coffee civilization, and yet again of a cocoa civilization. But in industrial society, professional autonomy and the culture of a trade or of a product melt away. Professional activity is increasingly defined directly in terms of the roles played in a communication system; psychologists have in fact begun to measure and evaluate qualifications in precisely such new terms. We need to add here that this communication network is itself not determined by technologies but increasingly by the state of professional relations within the organization.

The growing complexity of a programmed society can result only in a decreasing degree of integration. It corresponds to an organizational model that is much less simple, much less stable, and far less mechanical than that of preindustrial societies. We all feel it: our different experiences of participation in this society do not refer us back to one central point but rather to separate centers of decision that form a mosaic rather than a pyramid.

The sheer quantity of information and of the means of communication often leads to the assertion that our society can be defined as a communication society. Would it not be more accurate to say, however, that if it deserves such a name, it is because communication is one of its chief problems? Societies without massive means for the transmission of information were characterized by the correspondence between messages sent and social roles. In the extreme, communication was replaced with exchange, with the latter being socially, and even ritually, regulated between actors whose messages were in direct relation with their specific functions. In our society, a basic disjunction exists between communication in this sense and exchange. Information is defined less and less as exchange and more and more as sending, broadcasting—one could even say as advertising or propaganda if these words did not have such pejorative meanings. Information is increasingly tied to decision-making, that is, to power, to programming capability, and this in turn is associated with the growing power and costs of the means of communication. At the same time, understanding is rendered more difficult by the separation between information and social roles; as a result, it is sought between individuals defined independently of their social roles. Hence the importance given to nonverbal communication, to the search for direct contact, which impels people to equip their automobiles with C.B. radios in order to communicate with strangers. Aren't we all fascinated by the search for something that would not be a face-to-face encounter but a "voice-to-voice" one? And so we see in the large cities the appearance of voluntary telephone helplines to come to the assistance of potential suicides or anyone with a severe psychological problem. To be sure, radio and television give more and more space to talk shows, call-in shows, and games, but it is readily apparent that this is not enough to overcome the immense distance between the centralized broadcasting of information and the demand for interpersonal communication.

New Class Relations

Historicity—especially its most material form, namely investment—cannot be assumed by a "community." For a system to exist, there must be set up mechanisms of order, socialization, reproduction, social control, and repression. It is because these instruments of social order and of its maintenance are indispensable that historicity can be introduced only by one part or section of society, capable of freeing itself from the constraints of order, or, most often, of using them to its own advantage. The ruling class is the social group that takes charge of historicity, the specific actor that exerts the most general action on the workings and the transformation of society. The ruling class identifies itself with historicity and, at the same time, identifies it with its particular interests. It is "progressive'' inasmuch as it puts in motion a higher level of intervention of society upon itself and fights the older dominant categories and the older instruments of social control, but, on the other hand, it erects new barriers in the defense of its privileges.

What is, then, the nature of class relations in a programmed society? One is first tempted to say that the central social conflict pits directors against employees, those who invent, formulate, and direct the production programs against those who apply them and are subjected to them. Aren't we seeing a proletarianization of lower-level, then middle-level employees and even of "professionals" as once there was one of workers? Actually, this opposition between conceptual personnel and implementing personnel defines only a stratification scale and thus authority relations. When one speaks of class relations, one means much more than that: the ruling class is the one that holds the power to direct the creation of cultural models and of social norms; the dominated class is the one that has access to historicity only in a subordinated way by submitting to the role granted to it by the ruling class, or, on the contrary, by seeking to destroy this ruling class's appropriation of historicity.

If the specificity of the ruling class in the programmed society is the capacity to create models of social consumption, the ruled class cannot be defined as all of those who execute and implement these models, but as those who must conform to them. Even if the word may be dangerous, one must say, in order to underscore the distance that separates programmed society from industrial society, that the principal social conflict is the one that opposes the large production and management apparatuses to consumers. That is why the first manifestations of the new social conflicts have involved consumers in quite a spectacular way, or at least have appealed to them. Those who have spoken out against schools or against the university in the name of education, against the scientific-political complex in the name of public good, against hospitals in the name of health, against urban planning in the name of interpersonal relations, against the nuclear industry in the name of ecology, have always opposed what seems at first a matter of consumption against the influence of the great apparatuses upon the determination of demand. The power of such apparatuses must be called *technocratic*. And just as in an industrial society the ruling class is that of the *organizers*, be they public or private, one must avoid confusing the technocracy with the central administration of the State. There exists a private technocracy as much as a public one, a capitalist technocracy and a collectivist one. When they face technocracy, consumers speak in the name of their needs. The traditional thought of industrial societies has conceived needs as the simple replication of economic growth. Engel's famous laws meant to show that a rise in revenue augmented the share of optional consumption and lowered that of basic staples. Today we are seeing a violent rejection of this quantitative conception of needs, a rejection that takes the form of an appeal to deep, fundamental, and natural needs. Now, these are all notions that do not have a clear sociological meaning, but they are indicative of a will to oppose another mode of life and other preferences to the technocratic modeling of demand.

The specificity of the social conflict in a programmed society resides in the fact that the ruling class appears to hold sway over all of social life, a state of affairs that prevents the dominated from speaking and acting from the stronghold of a social and cultural autonomy. They are forced, then, to oppose social domination in the name of the only thing that may yet escape it, namely nature. This is what is important about the ecological movement, which appeals to life against a production ethic, pollution, and the dangers of nuclear contamination. It explains as well the importance of protest movements that rely upon a biological and not a social status: gender, youth, but also old age, membership in an ethnic group, and even in some measure, belonging to a local or regional culture insofar as language is not conceived as a simple product of society, since the same language can be used by a collectivity at different levels of social and economic organization. Such defensive actions can become utopian and result in the rejection of modern society if they are not linked to counteroffensive actions, that is, to the will to use modern science and technology in favor of countermodels of social and political organization. These countermodels may not be limited to the level of labor organization as was the case in industrial society. And since the idea of management has replaced that of organization, it is natural that the theme of self-management should replace that of socialism, that is, that of the workers' control over the organization of labor. But this defensive action and this counteroffensive action must be bound in some central location. In mercantile societies, this central locus of protest was called *liberty* since it was a matter of defending oneself against the legal and political power of the merchants and, at the same time, of counterposing to their power an order defined in legal terms. In the industrial epoch, this central locus was called *justice* since it was a question of returning to the workers the fruit of their labor and of industrialization. In programmed society, the central place of protest and claims is *happiness*, that is, a global image of the organization of social life on the basis of the needs expressed by the most diverse individuals and groups. It is clear, then, that the field of social struggles is no longer as clearly defined in programmed society as it was in its predecessors. In agrarian societies, it is always a matter of land; in mercantile societies, it is the citizen, the inhabitant, who is set into motion; in industrial society, it is the worker. And in programmed society, it is the social actor in any one of his or her roles—one could almost say that it is human being as living being. That is why we have protest movements in the name of everything, be it the individual taken as a bodily entity or in terms of projects to be achieved, or be it a community. But the very thing that seems to give social conflicts their exceptional extension and force in programmed society is also what makes for their weakness: the generalization of conflicts deprives them of a concrete central locus. Fire can be lit anywhere, but society seems less threatened than before by a great conflagration. That is perhaps why the future of social conflicts and movements depends very much in this society upon the intervention of political parties or upon the crisis of the State.

Stateless Societies or Societyless States

Isn't this view of programmed society too much on the prudent side? Some twenty years ago, when industrial society seemed to be winning out, it seemed imprudent to imagine that it could be rapidly replaced by another type of society. Today the notion of a postindustrial society is being generally abandoned because it appeared to have been linked to the optimism of this period and become reduced as a result to the image of a hyperindustrial society that did not lay a solid ground for the idea of societal change. The present crisis in industrial values leads to the formulation of an opposite reproach to the idea of a programmed society: this idea lags behind transformations that are already visible. But then the critics separate, with two divergent sets of analyses being opposed to the descriptions I have first advanced.

For some, as I indicated earlier, what is coming to an end is not a stage of growth but growth itself and, with it, the idea of development. The extreme capacity of societies to intervene upon themselves makes it impossible for them to pursue the "destructive creation" through which industrial society had defined itself according to Schumpeter. For a long time a finite capacity of action has existed in an environment that seemed finite; today we are in an altogether different situation: our capacity to act seems to exceed the resources that it can mobilize. So shouldn't a concern with survival and with equilibrium take over that with progress? Isn't it high time to recognize that humans are not located in front of nature but in it? The most extreme form taken by this questioning of present values is an appeal to return to an exchange or a barter society, a society without historicity. Some anthropologists, like Marshall Sahlins,[4] have even spoken of a return to plenty, showing that our industrialized societies rest on scarcity, whereas the societies of the Great Plains of North America know how to maintain their equilibrium by comsuming or ceremoniously destroying available surplus. Others, like Pierre Clastres,[5] have wished for a return to stateless societies. For a decade, we have heard wishes expressed to stop growth and to restore their lost importance to lived experience, direct exchange, the bodily and the local collectivity. At the same time, the chief theme of protest, which hitherto had been formulated in terms of social relation, property, or power, seemed to be concentrating around the actors, their identities, and their differences. These two notions played a central role in all the countercultural movements, in the women's movement as well as in those of ethnic and national groups.

This position lends itself to at least two criticisms. The first is that this appeal to community could lead to the acceptance of ever stronger constraints, because a society can cancel its historicity and limit itself to reproduction only through the operation of powerful social controls. One would need a Sparta far more rigorous than the actual one to prevent investment, the progress of knowledge and to reduce production to an integration that could rapidly transform itself into constraining obligations.

Second, the idea of limitations to growth has been linked to a very short period of our history, a period in which the overcoming of industrial society appeared to combine with plenty. This period ended at the beginning of the seventies in the United States and a little later in Western Europe. The study of student milieux is enlightening here. Since roughly 1975, the blossoming of countercultural models and of social and political utopias has come to an abrupt end, giving way to defensive behavior and concern about one's professional future. This does not mean that the questioning of industrial society should be abandoned, but that it is impossible to maintain for a long time the separation of cultural critique from political and social critique. The critique of a culture must transform itself into a critique of the social forces that are taking the reins of a new type of society. And this does not lead to a rejection of growth but to the need for imagining new forms of collective reappropriation for the instruments and the products of this new growth.

The notion of a programmed society has also been attacked from an opposite point of view, as presupposing the existence of a civil society and therefore of specifically social relations. Don't you see, say these critics, that this image held some reality for a very short time and in a very small part of the world? The civil society episode is coming to an end, and once again it is the State and the whole ensemble of mechanisms for the imposition and the maintenance of social order that will rule the day everywhere. The reason for this critique is easy to see. The great hope of industrial society was borne by the labor movement, which named socialism the societal model it opposed to capitalist society. But historically this societal model, which bore the hope of liberation for workers, has been incarnated in a totalitarian State the logic of which is that of absolute power and not at all the defense of the oppressed. As a result, the critique of the communist model, which some would like to call, by prudence, the Stalinist model in order to limit its field of application, has led some to conceive of all industrialized societies, and not only of the communist ones, as dominated by a State order. Instead of seeking to analyze new conflicts and new social movements, they have stressed repression, ideological inculcation, and confinement. This did have the effect of bringing to light a large number of social phenomena that had remained rather shadowy until now, but it also risks falsifying social analysis inasmuch as this view appears to exclude the possibility of conflicts and struggles in contemporary society. The best answer to this second critique is the growing disjunction between social relations and civil society and the State. It is true, and it is prob-

ably the most important phenomenon on the global scale, that an increasing number of countries are entering, in accelerated fashion and in a voluntarist mode,
the process of industrialization. The more voluntary this process, the less it is directed by social forces that have not yet become fully constituted, and the more
it is given over to the direction of a national or a foreign State.

The contemporary world is far more directed by States than was the case with
the Western countries on the way to industrialization during the nineteenth century. But, once again, this phenomenon is not of the same nature as the passage
from industrial society to programmed society. It is not accurate to speak of
power elites, of State monopoly capitalism, or of State bourgeoisie. On the contrary, one must separate more and more the analysis of the State from that of civil
society. Even in a country like France, haven't we seen the development of the
great technocratic apparatuses continue undisturbed through the upheavals of the
State, from the weak State of the Fourth Republic to the industrializing State of
the present day, and going through the properly statist phase of the State, concerned with sovereignty and grandeur during the de Gaulle years? The weaker
the integration of civil society, the more it is constituted by a multiple network of
decision centers and fields of social influence, a situation that increases the separation of the State from society. For the sphere of the State is that of historical
change, that is, of the preservation of the identity of a social aggregate caught
between its past and its future and threatened by other, surrounding, aggregates,
whereas civil society is a set of complex social relations punctured in ever more
places by conflicts and negotiations. The illusion of a return to equilibrium, just
like that of the devouring State, serves only to postpone the analysis of the new
ruling forces, of the new protest movements, and of the stakes in their conflicts.

The break between industrial society and its successor is not as complete,
then, as some had thought. We will not see new "primitive" societies springing
up; nor will we see social problems transmuted into political ones, except in
those places where authoritarian States rule the day. The society we are entering
in is defined, like its predecessors, by the labor it exerts upon itself and which,
through class relations, elaborates the categories of its practice. Exchange societies were followed by manufacturing societies; we now see emerging communication societies. What is radically new about them is that their capacity to act
upon themselves reaches all levels of economic activity and, as a result, they no
longer conceive of themselves as subordinated to a transcendental order of social
phenomena. A programmed society cannot acknowledge any order above itself.
Nor can it acknowledge the existence of a nature from which it would be separate. That is why it acknowledges that it is part of nature but, at the same time,
that it belongs to the social order. On the other hand, it acknowledges no other
gods than itself since it has the capacity to make itself over almost completely
and even to destroy itself. The specificity of a communication society lies in the

fact that it can and must be studied in terms of social relations. The meaning of the behavior of the actors is not to be found in principles, in the order of the universe, or in the meaning of history; it is nowhere but in the social relations of which the actor is a part. For the first time, the analysis of society must be directly sociological. This means also that since the whole set of mechanisms of social control and of socialization can no longer be represented as respecting natural laws or the preservation of traditional precepts, it will appear as increasingly repressive. Everything that appears to be objective, established, institutional, is shown, in this type of society, to be an obstacle to social relations, to communication. This justifies the importance of the critiques addressed against the State in social thought today. Programmed society is necessarily also a society of protest, of imagination, and of utopia, because it is wholly traversed by the social conflict between apparatuses with the capacity and the power to program, and the appeal to a creativity and a happiness constantly threatened by the logic of these apparatuses.

Sociology itself cannot simply wonder about the nature of society; it must uncover and describe social situations and the social relations hidden behind seemingly administrative or technical categories. It is in this sense that particular care must be taken not to define this as a technical society nor to name it after some of its technological instruments. On the contrary, this society must be represented as a field of conflictual social relations, which may lead to political breaks or to negotiations that result in relatively stable compromises. It is thus that the new features of a natureless society will become apparent, without a nature because it is entirely the product of the labor it exerts upon itself.

Chapter 11
The New Social Conflicts

In this chapter, I choose to disengage myself as much as possible from a global historical situation in order to bring to light "facts pregnant with the future." The danger in this position is obvious. No one thinks that any national society has presently turned into an actual postindustrial society. The very hesitation as to the name to be given to the new type of society is a clear indication that it cannot be internally defined. Some may fear that we are about to write some sociology-fiction. The danger is actually an opposite one. All those who are interested in the transformation of individual societies know they generally turn out to have been shortsighted: in order to avoid the traps of the imagination, they remain far too beholden to industrial reality. An example may suffice to bring this danger into focus: on all sides there is talk of the increasingly dominant role of multinational corporations. But practical observation does not help us to define a postindustrial society and to determine what differentiates it from an industrial one since these corporations belong to categories that are historically quite diverse, ranging from the old colonial ones to I.B.M., which relies upon modern information technology.

One must therefore run some risks in order to avoid others. One must not seek to isolate in a given realm of social reality, that of conflicts, for example, some purported modern "trend." One must always seek to tie as directly as possible the object of one's study to the most central aspects of a societal type: going at a remove from social organization and its workings in order to set up an analytical scheme that implies some consequence for a given realm of social reality. That is why I shall limit myself here to the presentation of four general propositions that define the nature of social conflicts in a new society.

1. In a Postindustrial Society, Conflicts Are Generalized

This society sees the disappearance, at the same time, of the sacred and of the traditional. This is not a new theme, nor should it be. The idea of postindustrial society intervenes here only as the renewed and more self-conscious form of the ancient theme of industrialization or even of modernization. In the past, actual social claims and protest were disjointed because they always fought an actual social opponent but appealed at the same time to the representative of a metasocial order. Dependent laborers fought their masters, their landlords, or the merchants but called upon the justice of the priest or that of the king. Workers fought against capitalism, but socialism is also an appeal to a national State as quasi-natural agent of historical development. Furthermore, every social movement, as agent of social conflict, has always linked its oppositional action to the image of a reunited community that would permit human beings to flourish, and which would bring about the free development of the forces of production, achieve national unity, defend common good, and so on. Conflicts, at least the most basic ones, the least negotiable, have generally been associated with the representation of a social nature freed from conflicts, the embodiment of a metasocial order within the social order. By the same token, every society maintained a preserve, a realm sheltered from social conflicts. Aren't we still beholden to the theme of the sacredness of science, the preserve of industrial society, equally appealed to by the Right and the Left, capitalists and socialists?

Not only is this sacredness disappearing, but it is invaded by the most basic of conflicts: instead of a higher world of unity, what is emerging is a central stake of the social conflicts. A symbolic aspect of this generalization of conflictuality is the withering away of the dream of a classless and conflict-free society. In the socialist world every step forward seems to be a step away from the ultimate community. Class conflicts, it has been said in China, continue in socialist society; in France, one speaks only of a society in transition to socialism.

The counterpart of the disappearance of the sacred is the vanishing of tradition, that is, not only of what is transmitted from the past, but of the rules of social and cultural organization based upon the preservation or the survival of the collectivity: disappearance of exchange systems, weakening or crisis of the mechanisms of social reproduction. Education was recognized simultaneously as an agent for the transmission of a given cultural heritage and as a mechanism of adaptation to professional and social change. The first of these functions has grown much weaker, and protests rise against an education that is seen both as archaic and as an instrument for the inculcation of dominant norms. This example, too well-known to warrant lengthy discussion, is important because it shows that conflicts have penetrated an immense realm which had seemed until now alien to social conflicts, that of "private life": family, education, sexual relations.

The decline of the sacred and of tradition and the generalization of conflicts are progressively weakening, at times in spectacular fashion, the role of the *intelligentsia*, defined as the set of educated people that serve as mediators between categories excluded from the political system and this system.

A postindustrial society tends to be a mass society, that is, to have achieved a generalized "mobilization" of the population. The rapid development of information and communication proper to postindustrial society weakens the role of intermediaries. The idea, which feminism spread widely and which has been adopted in even more extreme fashion by most of the nationalist and revolutionary movements of the Third World, that social demands must be assumed by a political party in order to break out from the dependency they are locked in, seems now to lag behind the practice of industrialized societies. Although base level movements and appeals to spontaneity have other causes and may, for this reason, prove to be of short duration, they seem to be the signs of a more enduring transformation: the rapprochement between the social base of a collective action and its means of action at the level of the society. This observation does not prejudge the forms of the political system, but it does point to the decline of the mediating party. Protest claims put into question directly the general orientations of the society, whether they emanate from a reformist interest group or are the activity of a revolutionary force. This explains why those in power are increasingly sensitive to "public opinion": this rather vague term actually designates a set of pressure and interest groups, and increasingly autonomous conflicts.

This sensitivity may give the powerful a feeling of insecurity, on the part of the powerful, and therefore lead to an accelerated development of propaganda, repression, and ideological controls. It can also lead to the growing openness of the political system and to a decentralization of decision-making. The confrontation between centralized power and base movements does not imply by itself either the weakening or the strengthening of the political system. Its importance derives from the fact that it indicates the generalized appearance of social movements that do not form at the level of a political collectivity but at that of the social problems themselves. The internationalism of the labor movement was an early indication of this phenomenon, But the tendency toward the autonomization of social movements with respect to their political expression—the counterpart of which we will see later—acquires a much greater importance as it is reinforced by the role of the mass media, which take the place of the intelligentsia and of properly political mediations.

2. In the Face of an Increasingly Integrated Power Complex, Opposition Tends to be Carried Out by Increasingly Global Groups

This proposition is an extension of the previous one. The main conflicts were always linked to the metasocial realm that seemed to rule over society. The idea that the economy is dominant in society located basic conflicts in the realm of labor, in the same way that in the society that came before industrial society, the preeminent role of political sovereignty endowed with central importance conflicts about citizenship and civil rights. There seems to exist in every society a privileged social role with which basic conflicts are in correspondence.

This state of affairs ceases to obtain in a society no longer defined by its subjection to a metasocial order but by its modes of action upon itself. Social domination no longer locates itself in a specific realm but inhabits them all. In this type of society an authoritarian regime can become totalitarian, though nothing forces such a society to have an authoritarian regime. Everywhere a mode of global management is being put into place in a way that cannot be reduced to an economic policy. Countries that think they can undergo an economic transformation while keeping forms of social organization inherited from the past, risk not being able to advance far into postindustrial society. This is happening to Western Europe, which is sufficiently modern economically to enter into the mobility of American society but not so socially to become an autonomous center of development.

The gap is closing between social control and social management as it becomes more and more a question of administering human beings. The social sciences have already given rise to technologies, particularly economic ones, in which planning and forecasting rely upon much better economic information, shedding light upon decisions that may even have gone through a simulated stage. But even in the properly social realm, we find the same influence, as authority relations, or those that obtain in education, are being transformed through the intervention of social scientists. Just because large corporations have often resorted to caricatural forms of psychosociological intervention should not lead us to think that the latter does not work or is no more than an ideological smokescreen. One of the clearest lines of demarcation between industrial and postindustrial society is the one separating the view that technology, considered as productive, should be disjoined from culture, viewed as reproductive, from the notion that technical ''factors'' and human factors are interdependent. The critique of taylorized rationalization, formulated early in this century, and the development of occupational sociology have had, and continue to have, a very great importance by slowly forcing a mode of analysis in terms of organizations and not of enterprises or business (conceived as either purely economic entities or technical forms of production). These few remarks have no other goal than to explain the central transformation of social conflicts. The great social struggles cannot be carried out in the name of the citizen or of the worker against a domination apparatus that increasingly subjects all of society to its management so that it may orient it to a given type of development; it has to be in the name of collectivities defined more by their being than by their activity. The reversal with respect to past societies is obvious. *Negotium* was the basis for the protests of popular categories against the *otium* of the ruling class; today this class is *negotium*, technocracy, and no longer a leisure class. Conversely, the groups that are subjected to social domination begin by mounting a global resistance against manipulation. Against a global form of domination, resistance cannot be confined in one social role; it becomes important only if it mobilizes the entire collectivity.

Students can now play an important role because the sharp rise in their number and the increased duration of studies have resulted in the constitution of student collectivities with their own space, capable of opposing the resistance of their own culture and of their personal concerns to the space of the large organizations that seek to impose themselves even more directly upon them. In another realm, the problems of the workplace are far from eliminated, but they are now part of a larger whole, within which they no longer can play the central role that used to be theirs. It is useless to search for indications of revolutionary renewal that would be specifically of working-class origin. Where it is most combative, as in Italy and in France, the workers' movement can gain, through conflicts and crises that may become violent, an extension of rights and of the capacity to negotiate, and thus a certain institutionalization of labor conflicts. The Communist and Socialist parties in these countries progressively turn into "republican" or "democratic" movements, in analogy with the end-of-century Radical parties, and they have as a goal the incorporation within the political system of social categories currently sacrificed. Goldthorpe and his collaborators have shown quite well that this does not mean that the working class is becoming more bourgeois;[1] nor does it indicate the preservation or the simple renewal of the labor movement. The latter simply stops being a central character of social history as one gets nearer to postindustrial society.

One could go as far as observing that most of the social movements on the stage of history today draw upon "transmitted status" and not upon "ascribed status." We speak of the women's movement, the youth movement, or of those of Blacks, Native Peoples, or of the inhabitants of a region, a country, or even a continent.

It would be a mistake to think that one goes from social movements to countercultural movements. The phrase is too vague and rests upon an interpretation—which I consider false—of the signification of the events of May 1968. One must not confuse the emergence of utopias of a new sort with social movements. These new utopias are important, however, because they do indicate the direction in which the new social movements will form.

3. Social Conflicts and Marginal or Deviant Behavior Tend to Become Conflated

As a general management apparatus imposes itself upon the whole of society, oppositional forces will appear as minorities. One speaks naturally of the silent majority, and not only in countries in which opposition is subject to direct repressive measures, like the Soviet Union, but also in politically liberal capitalist countries. At the same time, and especially in the United States, all oppositional or resistance forces are covered by the term *minority,* which we see equally applied to Blacks, Chicanos, Native Americans, gays, lesbians, and even to women who are in a minority position in higher-level or better-paid professions. This reversal is astonishing, as spectacular as that of *negotium* and *otium.* Not long ago, power holders were designated as monarchs of oligarchs. One spoke of the fifty, or the two hundred, families. And there is little doubt about the nature of recent economic concentration, since those who run the large businesses with multinational operations hold ever larger power. However, as the management of technico-social systems gains in importance, social integration becomes an essential instrumentality of power. I am not concerned here with societies that are mobilizing in order to make good their belatedness and to come out of their dependency. I limit myself, on the contrary, to the most advanced societies, of the Western type, which do not have to carry out this kind of ideological and political mobilization. In their case integration does not come from the top, from the center of decisions, but from the bottom: consumption sets up hierarchies and achieves integration by multiplying indices of social standing. Within organizations themselves, other forces of integration are at work. All the members of these ensembles which are at the core of society partake of the power of the system, not only through higher salaries, but also through greater job security, career opportunities, and other benefits. Some individuals rebel against this integration, especially in the name of private initiative or of technical rationality in the case of managerial personnel, but most are quite appreciative of the protection represented by the large corporation or its equivalent. Opponents are not to be found among those who decide to break with these organizations and their advantages—an aristocratic reaction of decidedly limited scope—but foremost among those who are swallowed up by the power of these organizations or who feel their hold. In many cases, the large organization imposes an image of normativity, of centrality, and thus constitutes marginal groups by the imposition of its rules.

One of the most important examples, and still not studied enough, is that of health. Everywhere we find a tendency to "medicalize" social problems. A child's difficulties in school could be explained by her or his social origin or by the nature of educational norms; instead there are powerful forces that intervene to make this child appear to be sick. Now this may seem to represent a progressive reaction in relation to more brutal ones, such as accusing the child of laziness or asserting that the child lacks intelligence, but we must recognize that what is involved here is a mechanism for reducing social problems to problems of marginality. All one need do is push this tendency to the extreme, and one begins to lock up political opponents in psychiatric hospitals.

The reduction of conflict to marginality leads in turn to the reinterpretation of marginality in terms of conflict. We have seen antipsychiatry put the definition of madness as deviance into question, and some interpretations go so far as to identify madness with a desire and a libido that have been repressed and crushed by the social organization. What is more interesting yet is to see the appearance of protest and of conflict where formerly only the repression of deviance was to be found. Prison rebellions, frequent in many countries, exceed the simple challenge to conditions of confinement. The notion of social order, which tends to be imposed everywhere, is revealed, at the same time, to be directly linked to dominant ideology, and is challenged as a result. This brings us back to an earlier theme: conflict is no longer associated with a sector considered basic to social activity, to the infrastructure of society, and especially to the workplace; it is everywhere. Just as the distinction between productive and nonproductive no longer has any meaning, that of the various "instances" (the economic, the political, the ideological) also loses all usefulness. When fundamental conflicts appear in all the realms of social life, however, there is no longer a clear separation between conflicts and other nonconforming behavior. Perhaps this separation was linked to the negotiated phase of labor conflicts and thus to the "responsible attitude" of labor unions and parties. But, it seems to me, the observed evolution is less dependent on conjunctural factors. The farther one goes into the past, the greater the distance between opposition forces, which are primarily the new rising ruling classes on one side, and the excluded forces, considered as impure, criminal outgroups on the other. Aren't we presently going through a reverse movement, that is, the mixing of opponent and deviant, something that is logical as soon as the dominant group imposes an order and a normativity on all society?

This changes profoundly the usual image of social conflicts. From the industrial era we have inherited the image of two opponents, the capitalists versus the working class, confronting each other on a ground and with weapons that are those of the ruling class, to be sure, but which do not prevent the confrontation from being a direct one. Today, on the contrary, the image that prevails is that of an impersonal and integrating central apparatus that controls, beyond a "service class," a silent majority, and scattered around the latter are a number of excluded, confined, underprivileged, or even denied, minorities.

One could imagine the erection of ghettos to which the categories rejected by segregation would be confined and within which there would develop subcultures, all still dependent upon the central core. The youth communities that multiplied at a given time are characteristic of the ambiguity of these "marginals"; they are loci of global protest and opposition, but also places of voluntary retreat and dependence. Aren't young and old, defined by their nonparticipation in large organizations, to be found organized in marginal settlements of this type? Intellectuals, deprived of their role as the intelligentsia, similarly tend to challenge the social order while contributing to its preservation by their very marginalization. It seems to be increasingly difficult to apprehend directly "pure" basic conflicts. Everything is getting mixed up, marginality and exploitation, defense of the past and claims upon the future.

4. Structural Conflicts and Conflicts Tied to Change Are Diverging

On most of the globe problems of developments hold sway over all others; societies are being defined by the way in which they are changing from one societal type to another, more than by specific problems of one sort or another. In industrialized societies, reality runs in reverse. Although they are undergoing rapid transformations, they live more and more in the synchronic dimension. This is linked to the extension of the political system and to the development of mass culture and mass society. This, in turn, led to a recognition of the limits of growth, an essential theme since it marks a rupture with the historicism and the evolutionism of the past century to which we still paid allegiance. It is therefore increasingly difficult for us to define oppositional forces as bearing a new power: the opposition must define itself as such, without carrying within itself a model of society and the seed of a new State. The lower class cannot be identified with a new type of ruler. We are finding out that class conflicts are no longer instruments of historical change. This explains why we have come across resistance and defense forces rather than a counteroffensive capability, a conflictual situation rather than conflicts. Groups on the defensive were usually drawn into a counteroffensive either by a new ruling class or by a political and ideological elite. As they remain independent, don't the forces of conflict risk staying on the defensive permanently, while the apparatus reigns like the sun in the midst of society? Isn't it striking to see that in the part of the world where opposition is not stifled, it occurs piecemeal, without the possibility of seeing the emergence of a general social movement analogous to the labor movement as it existed in the preceding period? By contrast, in the rest of the world, the domination of the great empires causes the State to be the chief agent of opposition as soon as the national collectivity is independent.

This type of collective mobilization, which is meant to allow a country to cross over into a new stage in spite of the obstacles standing in the way of its progress, and especially in spite of the dependency it is experiencing, is not of the same nature as the social movements that form without a postindustrial type of society. By the same token, we must not confuse the labor movement, structural opposition to capitalism, and revolutionary or conservative State action for the voluntary industrialization of a dependent or underdeveloped country.

Under these types of conditions it is not possible for an ideologically coherent set of social movements to acquire a principle of unity that would qualify it as manager. What unites oppositional social movements can only be their oppositional attitude. Their critical action, constantly trying to break the crust of ideologies, of the categories of practice and of roles in order to recover not spontaneity or human nature but the reality of social relations, is the only possible principle of unity for the forces of opposition and of resistance in the type of society we are entering. These societies are doomed to be authoritarian, to become apparatuses, if they are not transformed by this critical activity—an elementary condition of democracy. In front of the sovereign, democracy was political; facing capitalism, it became "social," that is, it learned to enter the realm of labor and became industrial democracy. In the face of ruling apparatuses that increasingly hold sway over all aspects of social life, democracy can only be global, cultural in the sense given to the term when we spoke of cultural revolution. Conflict must now be introduced and recognized in all realms of social life and especially at the level of social and cultural organization, in other words, of established order. Wherever there exists an order, there must be a challenge to this order. This challenge will be desultory if it aims to create a parallel counter-order—as occurred with the so-called critical university in France, which became more dogmatic than the regular ones—but basic if it reminds us that order covers up interests, conflicts, and the stakes in them. Aren't we seeing the social agencies traditionally devoted to the formation and the transmission of the social and cultural order, such as schools, the Church, and even the family, sometimes become places of refuge and more and more often places of protest? The emergent conflicts are increasingly directed against the "infrastructures," or, to speak more simply, against order, since the new power has a capacity hitherto unknown of endowing itself with the appearance of order and of dominating an entire social organization and its categories of social practice, instead of locking itself up in castles, palaces, or financial districts. We are entering into a type of society that can no longer "have" conflicts: either these are repressed within the framework of authoritarian order, or the society acknowledges itself as conflict, indeed is conflict, because it is nothing more than the struggle of opposed interests for the control of the capacity to act upon itself.

This unity of oppositional movements is strengthened by a more positive unifying mechanism: political action. This is a direct consequence of the previously mentioned separation of social movement and party. As soon as the social movement is no longer the base or the raw material of the action of the party, which alone is a bearer of meaning, we must reverse the relation and recognize that social movements come into being and integrate within each other only inasmuch as they relate to political forces that in no way represent them but base their strategy upon them. Popular social movements can become organized only within a "Left " political strategy, but such movements are now, and will be even more in the future, independent of political parties. The latter fail if they are ideological; the former become divided and scatter if they are not strategically unified, not brought together by properly political, and therefore instrumental, objectives, in relation to which they keep their freedom, and even a certain oppositional role. As a result, the form of the action undertaken by social movements increasingly depends upon the features of the political system.

On the other hand, however scattered they may be, social movements are the bearers of a global meaning, of an image of the society, and they are not confined to the limited world of protest, claims, and reforms. If the political system is closed, that is, subjected to some despotism, social movements break up and ultimately become confused with marginal or deviant behavior. The relative importance of baseline social movements and of their integration at a properly political level depends above all on the degree of disjunction between problems of development and problems of functioning in the postindustrial society. As a consequence, the easier the entry of a society into this societal type, the greater the role of the political system and of its components, a state of affairs that favors a great diversification of base movements, in the spirit of a grass-roots democracy. When obstacles to entry into a postindustrial society are greater, political institutions have less autonomy with respect to the State or with respect to the foreign bourgeoisie that directs development, and oppositional movements are unified by an ideology of social opposition far more than by a political strategy. These two instances correspond perhaps to the classical opposition of such modern societies as Sweden, the United States, Germany, and even Great Britain, and of still very heterogeneous societies with large archaic sectors, like France and Italy.

The dominant idea in the various hypotheses I have formulated is easy to summarize: a postindustrial society, being nothing more than what it does, and being freed from all recourse to essences, turns completely into a field of conflicts. These may or may not be negotiated or limited, depending upon the state of the political collectivity in question and its institutions. This idea runs counter to the belief that increases in personal wealth will appease conflicts, and even more so against the opinion—too superficial to warrant discussion—that all "great conflicts" will be reduced to a multitude of tensions, strategies, and very empirical negotiations aimed solely at the management of change.

It is essential to posit the existence of a societal type and to analyze its structural conflicts. One may reject the separation between industrial and postindustrial society which I accept here, but one cannot consider that the only problem of the most industrialized societies is the management of change. Problems of power and of social domination have not disappeared, and structural conflicts are in fact spreading, as the realm of the sacred melts away in the heat of planned or organized transformations.

Chapter 12

The Ebbing of Social Movements

In the early 1970's, our societies witnessed an invasion by new social movements that challenged the forms of power characteristic of an advanced industrial society or even of a postindustrial one. After the blows struck by students first at Berkeley, then at Nanterre, came the ecological and the antinuclear movements, consumer associations, health self-management groups, feminist associations, and the women's liberation movement. The changes taking place in social reality had an impact upon sociological thought and led many sociologists to grant central importance to the notion of social movement.

For some time now it would seem that these facts and ideas are becoming part of the past. The economic crisis, the severity of international confrontations, as well as the virulence of collective movements far removed from those the West had become familiar with in the sixties, in Iran on one side and in Poland on the other—all lead to a turning away from opinion trends that, for their part, are losing steam and hesitate between isolation and an all-too-easily exercised influence. Reflection on society increasingly turns into analysis of the State, of its economic policy, and of its role in international competition. Soon perhaps the only theme that will hold our attention will be that of world peace or of war. There are already those who think that the recent social movements, which only a few years ago seemed to hold so much promise for the future, were actually only the last fires of an era come to the end, that of reckless expansion linked to Western hegemony over most of the planet.

Since I count myself among those who granted importance to these new social movements and who wanted to draw from a reflection upon their action a new conception of sociology, I must cast a critical glance upon the facts and ideas I thought so important. Did we perhaps exaggerate the scope of phenomena that were ultimately ephemeral and of little import? Wasn't there perhaps at the root of an overly complacent attention to minor phenomena a fear of the great upheavals that were transforming the world and that had little relation to the state of mind of intellectuals belonging to the middle class of the richest countries in the world?

Whatever answer we may give to these questions and critiques, it is impossible today to be satisfied with a voluntarist description of these new social movements; we must reflect upon the difficulties they encountered, the reasons for their decline and perhaps for their disappearance.

In any case, the sociologists who posited the existence of the new social movements were too quick to identify the particular actions they observed with a general model. Thus they underestimated the importance of circumstances that were quite peculiar, for at least two reasons. On the one hand, these struggles were being carried out in an exceptional economic period, at the end of a long phase of economic expansion marked by a belief in the capacity of industrial societies, especially of the Western type, for indefinitely continuing to grow richer and more complex. On the other hand, these struggles were not inseparable from ideologies of an altogether different nature, calling into question the domination exerted by a central economico-political power not only over Western societies themselves but also and, most of all, over the whole world. The student rebellions in the United States, Japan, Germany, Italy, and France in the sixties cannot be understood without a reference to the great movement against the war in Vietnam, a movement which spread then throughout these countries. This anticapitalist, anti-imperialist, and anticolonialist orientation was often quite removed from the themes of the new social movements, especially in the United States: what did the Free Speech Movement at Berkeley in 1964 have in common with the ideology of the S.D.S. at Columbia, or later with that of the Weathermen? A similar opposition is equally visible in the France of 1968 with a cultural opening up, emergent social movements, and leftist ideology getting mixed up and mutually reinforcing one another without eliminating what opposed them.

The authors of these studies are entitled to answer that the weakness of their analyses was inevitable. Marx could not take into account the particular conditions of capitalist industrialization in England when he elaborated his general theory of capitalism on the strength of the English example alone, and this for the excellent reason that at the moment when he was thinking it out, the British example was by far the most important, and virtually the only one, he could observe. Similarly, in the sixties what mattered most was to apprehend the actors and the new field, of social struggles. Whether one accepts or rejects this justification, however, the fact remains that today one can no longer be content with overly simple identification of a particular social structure with a specific historical conjuncture, and one must therefore learn to separate the general from the particular and transitory in what is called social movements. This is the more necessary because the great protest themes did not lead to the formation of new or important political actions. Whereas the workers' movement, and especially unionism, were quickly accompanied by the rise of socialist groups, movements, and parties, one must acknowledge that so far the new social movements have led only to the formation of weak ecological parties—except in Germany—and to the candidacy of some feminists for public office, who generally received far fewer votes than their influence in public opinion suggested. One must therefore reflect first of all upon the limits of a particular historical conjuncture and upon the ebbing away of the social movements with the end of this conjuncture, and then ask onself if the crisis is only conjunctural or whether it puts the very existence of social movements into question.

Decomposition of Social Movements

Historians of the workers' movement have often insisted upon the opposition between two types of periods which correspond to different phases of the economic situation. Periods of expansion are more favorable to the formation of social and cultural movements, whereas crisis or recession stages favor political action in the strict sense of the term. Similarly today, after decades during which everything was a question of basic cultural changes and ground-level initiatives, the reversal of the economic situation leads us to be far more concerned with economic policy, with decision-making ability at the top, and with the role of the State. This hold of the political over the social, and even more over the cultural, manifests itself in two different ways, which one must clearly separate but whose consequences frequently intersect.

The most spectacular form of the dominance of social action by political action is terrorism since the latter forms at the junction of older social movements, which have become more ideological than practical, with reactions to a crisis of the State. The recent terrorist movements, like the anarchist actions of the nineteenth century, occur at the moment when a certain type of society, and the social movements that pertain to it, are dying out. Whereas organized labor's system of claims is highly institutionalized, intellectuals or isolated militants attempt to use violence to create a breach in the social order that would revive mass action. By itself, terrorism, like a guerrilla organization in another context, is quite the opposite of a class and a mass action: it marks the extreme disjunction between the theoretical appeal to an already vanished movement and very institutionalized claims. But this ideological component results in action only when it is associated with crisis behavior, that is, with the calling into question of the social order itself, and thus of the State which is its representative and its guarantor. The rise in terrorism has found especially broad support in Italy, where other movements, in the urban realm in particular, had shown the vulnerability of public order. In Germany as well, though in a different manner, one cannot divorce terrorism from the awareness of a political crisis situation in which extreme Left views cannot find any legitimate way of being expressed politically. A counterexample is provided by France, where between 1970 and 1973 strong tendencies toward terrorism were stifled by the unity of the Left and the perspective of a favorable political outcome through electoral means. In other situations, and especially in Great Britain, the tendency to terrorism is absent because the political system remains open, and the ebbing of the social manifests itself mostly by the emphasis placed on the traditional ideological and political themes of the workers' movement on the Left in the Labour party and by the relatively important influence achieved by Communists and radical socialists in the unions.

At the opposite end of a situation that gives birth to terrorism, we find one in which social claims are institutionalized very early. In many countries, especially in those that have been most deeply affected by a social-democratic experience and are not going through a political crisis of the national State, protest movements readily turn into pressure groups, obtain legal measures that satisfy them by and large, while leaving behind some elements of protest that no measure can completely appease. In many countries the far-reaching institutionalization of labor claims has turned union activists and the vast majority of the workers into a defense force leading to new forms of social integration; the counterpart of this development is the marginalization of individuals and of groups, especially of the young unemployed whose anger formerly fueled the protest movements but which today is considered the expression of a marginality that rapidly borders on delinquency. This remark admits of generalization. In most European countries, which are dominated by State intervention and by various mechanisms for the institutionalization of conflicts, social movements tend to collapse into ''social problems'' if not into private ones. After the adoption of major laws responding to women's demands, the women's movement generally grew weaker while there proliferated groups concerned with bodily, or childbearing, experience or with the search for a female identity that is defined less and less in terms of conflict or of protest.

Whether violence carries the day or, on the contrary, an early institutionalization stands in the way of the formation of genuine social movement, one sees a gradual lessening of the initial impulse. Going even further, one could advance the proposition that if social movements exist only through the fact that adversaries have a common objective, then as soon as a society no longer refers to a metasocial principle of unity, such an objective cannot exist. Some observers, already referred to, conclude that conflicts are being dispersed. Others, on the contrary, assert that social struggles are turning into battles to the finish because the dominant actor achieves absolute domination and the dominated actor is reduced to exclusion. The age of societies and of social problems would then be over, and the State would be today the sole center of power and the only object of protest and challenge. Is this not the reason that, at the very moment when the idea and the reality of class struggle are growing weaker in the West, the theme of human rights regains its importance, reviving the traditional struggle of civil society led by intellectuals against the State and its military and police power? It is true indeed that on a world scale the Western countries' internal social struggles seem to be of little importance in relation to the actual, or virtual, struggles and passions that are elicited by the existence of dictatorial and even totalitarian States. We are coming here to the extreme point of the critique addressed to the analysis of the new social movements. It is no longer a question of criticizing only the shortsightedness of analysts and ideologues, and of showing that the circumstances of the eighties are not those of the sixties; it is not even a question of saying that some social movements are already exhausted while those that must succeed them have not yet come into being. This critique proclaims that it is high time to abandon conceptions inherited from past centuries and that everywhere in the world we live in, though under a great diversity of forms, an absolute State is taking the place of a ruling class, and that this means that properly social conflicts are being replaced henceforth by political ones; the struggle of the citizen against the State prevails today over that of the worker against his or her boss.

All these critiques raise questions and doubts that cannot be swept aside. But is it not possible to uphold a contrary thesis in the face of the present weakness of social movements, and to speak not of their decline or disappearance but of their slow and difficult birth?

Formation of Social Movements

Let us go back. What has been called the workers' movement is a far less simple reality than it appears at first. If one admits that the central social conflicts are located in the organization of labor, that is, at a particular level of social organization, one that is lower than that of the production of needs—which will be the historical center stage of postindustrial society—one must immediately acknowledge that labor action as such has been subordinated to political action in industrial society, meaning concretely the subordination of unionism to socialism. In a number of countries, the unity of the labor movement seemed to be borne only by the idea of revolution, that is, by the seizure of State power through violence, something that, by definition, can have only partial and complex relations with labor action, as the example of the Soviet Revolution makes abundantly clear. The labor movement, whose power is frequently evoked to underscore the weakness of the new social movements, is not really a wholly social movement. It is remarkable indeed that most analysts, speaking of the labor movement, do not speak of the struggle of the workers against the factory owners, but rather of that of the people against the capitalists, considered as the masters of money and not as the operators of factories. Only at a very recent date has attention been paid to the behavior of workers, whereas for a very long time the bulk of studies and ideologies have been concerned with the dominant role of the bourgeoisie in the industrialization process.

Today, as we enter postindustrial society, social movements can constitute themselves independently of any mixture, with political actions aiming at the direct seizure of State power. The chief feature of social movements today is to be purely social. This is why their alliance with cultural movements has been so spectacular and so fruitful; it is also why with the current return of the political they appear so weakened, whereas in industrial society the labor movement never appeared so strong as when social claims were transformed directly into political action. This novelty of the social movements of today is apparent in their very form. We are still used to the image of small core groups of militants animated, to be sure, by deep convictions but mostly capable of mobilizing the masses into political action, from direct confrontations with the police or the army to the capture of a governmental palace. The new social movements, on the contrary, are not formed through political action and confrontation but far more by influencing public opinion. They are diffuse, whereas the labor movement was concentrated. The very weakness of today's social movements must cause us to forget that they represent a large portion of public opinion. This weakness is easy to observe even in France, where the ecological and antinuclear movement received a very small percentage of votes in the elections it participated in, and where the government's pronuclear policy has gone from success to success for over ten years, with very powerful pronuclear arguments and with weak and disorganized antinuclear forces. In 1981 nearly 40 percent of the population expressed its opposition to the nuclear policy of the government, and a clear majority backed the holding of a national referendum on problems it considered to be of vital importance and the decisive power of which it recognized. It may be that the new social movements appear so weak because, consciously or not, we compare them with the same model of reference, the labor movement, the true meaning of which we pretend to forget. Quite the contrary, the women's movement and the ecological movement have rapidly won an audience and an influence far greater than those achieved by the labor union movement, and even all forms of labor action (cooperatives, credit unions, municipal actions, cultural actions, etc.) in the middle of the nineteenth century, dozens of years after the effects of the great capitalist industrialization began to be felt.

Having heard at length the critiques addressed to analysts of social movements, we now must regain the initiative and change the direction of our reflection to ask a less historical and a more sociological question than the one we have just considered: how can opinion movements coalesce, concentrate, and organize into collective actions capable of challenging the central forms of social domination and thus of turning into genuine social movements?

How can defense reactions in the face of a crisis be transformed into a social movement, going through a number of intermediate steps of collective action to be found at the level of social organization or at that of decision-making systems? It is difficult to imagine a revolt that could be immediately transformed into the central conflict; the rebelling force is too weak and subject to forces that marginalize it. It must begin by inserting itself into the social organization by building up its claim-making capability; it must then be able to change into a pressure group and exert some influence. If the revolt does not manage to insert itself in the workings of the society, it becomes a force of rupture, even a revolutionary agent, if the forces rejected by the social organization and the decision-making systems are powerful enough, and the established order is sufficiently shaken by an externally caused crisis. For present-day Western societies, a revolutionary outcome is not very probable, given the openness of decision-making and conflict-management systems. It behooves us, then, to reflect upon the factors that can favor or impede the transformation of revolts and refusals into organized claims and then into pressures of a political type, and ultimately into a social movement in the strict sense.

The passage from revolt or refusal behavior to claim-laying and demand-making presupposes both a relative openness of organizations and repressive action by the forces of social control. This combination of positive and negative elements must be found at all levels. If there is general repression, refusal behavior quickly turns into collective revolt, and the latter finds itself quickly propelled toward direct confrontation, with the group with the highest index of revolt being led to adopt extreme positions too quickly. The outcome is defeat through marginalization. Conversely, the absence of any repression and an openness of organizations one could consider "democratic" end with the incorporation of the claims in the functioning of these organizations. For a revolt to turn into a claim-making and demand-setting movement, it must both run against some resistance and then succeed in changing the way an area of social organization works; otherwise it begins to close upon itself.

The passage from claim-making to political pressure requires first of all some openness in the political system, and especially the intervention of political allies. At the end of the nineteenth century, workers' claims and union actions developed into the labor movement through the support of progressive political forces: republican, democratic, or radical parties, depending on the country. In addition, the claims made must be both negotiable and nonnegotiable, so that the claim-laying action is not swallowed up by the political system; then, strengthened by its very successes as well as by its protests, it remains in principle negotiable but nonintegrable into the existing political system.

Finally the passage from political pressure group to social movement also requires the intervention of an integrative factor and of a conflictual one. The main element of the conflict is a clear definition of the social opponent: the class consciousness and the action of the captains of industry were the most powerful factor in the constitution of the labor movement. On the other hand, no social movement will come into being if the actors in the conflict cannot identify with cultural values. The labor movement formed only when it went beyond the rejection of machines and began to defend the idea that mechanization and progress should be put in the service of workers and of all the people.

What is the present situation and how can the discontent of public opinion be transformed into a social movement? European societies are not very repressive, but the large production apparatuses have little flexibility, and this may lead the forces of discontent to a higher level of action. At that level—that of decision-making—the openness seems quite considerable today, especially in countries with mechanisms for the early institutionalization of new social conflicts. At the same time, the nonnegotiable sphere remains important, as is readily seen in antinuclear struggles and in the women's movement. It is easy, then, for emerging movements to express themselves at the political level, while keeping their autonomy as social forces. On the other hand, the transformation from political pressure forces into social movement is difficult. This is due first of all to the fact that the ruling technocrats have a low level of class consciousness because the mechanisms for the transition into postindustrial society are today more important and more visible than the functional mechanisms of this society. In addition, the role of the State is larger, and this results in a dangerous confusion between the realm of social relations, especially class relations, and that of State initiative. During the period of expansion, the class consciousness of the technocrats developed more rapidly, but the onset of crisis has provoked, among rulers and popular movements alike, a regression that pushes social conflicts to a lower level. Another difficulty comes from the fact that intellectuals are not giving a clear formulation of the stakes of the new struggles.

In the nineteenth century, from Saint-Simon and Auguste Comte to Herbert Spencer, the great themes of progress and evolution imposed themselves powerfully; today some intellectuals may well be constructing new models of knowledge and thus showing the novelty of investment mechanisms, but the most important tendencies in intellectual life are primarily concerned with the interpretation of past struggles and practices, so that quite often it seems as if intellectuals were opposed to the analysis of new social facts.

All of these observations lead to the conclusion that the present situation of Western industrialized societies is favorable to the emergence of protest movements, and even to their transformation into pressure groups, but that the moment of their passage to the level of social movements has not yet come. This is why we often see the joint presence of strongly institutionalized claim-making forces and nonnegotiable "emotional" residues, incapable of fueling by themselves a social movement. Conversely, it seems difficult for discontent to turn into revolt, and the latter into revolutionary movements in countries with broad political openness, as we can see even in Germany today, where the peace movement participates in political life and presents itself as a force for the renewal and extension of democracy even though it rests on a will to effect a radical political break. None of the present struggles can be designated as the principal conflict around which all others could gather. Political ecology does not have a more general meaning than the women's movement and, conversely, the latter seems incapable of asserting itself as a general movement that would mobilize men as well as women.

It is difficult, though, to be satisfied with the idea that the present struggles can only conclude alliances while remaining separate. The example of the sixties leads us to think, on the contrary, that the unification of the struggles can only be through increasingly closer ties between social struggles and cultural movements, because in a postindustrial society the stake in the action of the rulers as well as in that of opposition movements is the management of this society's capacity to act upon its members' behavior, their representation and their demands. The unification of the struggles or their integration in a general social movement can take place only through the reinforcement of their moral dimension, their will to apprehend and directly affirm the rights of the subject. Labor union action was essentially instrumental. It was directed against its opponents in order to liberate both the productive forces and the workers from the obstacles put in their way by capitalism. The labor movement worked for the future, a better tomorrow, for what Marx called the end of the prehistory of humankind. Today's social movements want to live immediately in conformity with what they believe social life should become. A spectacular form of the passage from one form of action to another was provided by the great popular demonstration of May 13, 1968, in Paris. It had been conceived as a traditional popular and labor demonstration at the moment when the student revolt was being taken over by the parties of the Left and by union organizations. A huge cortege of a million people crossed the city from north to south. But just as it was drawing to a close at the Place Denfert-Rochereau, the leading elements of the student rebellion, and especially its most popular leader, Daniel Cohn-Bendit, called on the demonstrators not to roll up their signs and go home but to gather on the Champ de Mars where a vast sit-in took place, a lived experience of the community wished for. The passage from linear march to circular gathering provides vivid illustration of the passage from a primarily instrumental action to a movement that is mainly exemplary and expressive. This is where the women's movement, in the strict sense, occupies most clearly a central position. Whereas feminism still belongs to a movement for civil rights conceived in the spirit of the Enlightenment and seeks to give women rights equal to those of men by eliminating discrimination and interdictions, the women's movement is wary of this equality in which it sees the risk of a dependency vis-à-vis the world of men. The women's movement, by breaking with the contradictions of an egalitarianism that ends up in ignoring the difference and the specificity of the female condition, retreats to a female community more or less openly lesbian, but, at the same time, it seeks to transform this voluntary confinement into the means for elaborating a relationship, between subjects, in which neither of the partners holds the meaning of the behavior of the other.

The more the new social struggles enter into the realms of culture and personality, the more they increase the chances of integrating the various struggles in a general social movement. But in order to succeed, this integration needs to be confronted with the action of external forces of resistance and repression. In an entirely "open" society, the integration of the various struggles could not be pushed to its end. The resistance comes primarily from the State, which opposes to the autonomy of social relations the pressing exigencies of international competition. In a period of crisis, this conflict between State and society can only grow more virulent.

Social Movements between Culture and Politics

The new social movements call into question, far more directly than their predecessors did, the values of culture and society, with a view to having these values rest directly upon intellectual and ethical convictions and not only on social ones. At the same time, the conditions of their action are more and more dependent upon the intervention of the State. As a result, social movements tend to oscillate between an ethics based on convictions and increasingly removed from concrete historical reality, and a logic of efficacy which leads them to submit to the influence of political actors. The tendency toward this split increases with the hold of the State over civil life; where the political system ensures a more autonomous and efficient mediation between State and social forces, social movements manage to better control the relation between action and conviction. This is why the political openness of countries with social-democratic regimes, instead of leading to the exhaustion of social movements, favors their integration and therefore their efficacy.

Today, however, far more important than the effects of the nature of the new social movements are those of a historical conjuncture that hesitates between the past and the future. Almost all of the new actors who have emerged, especially since 1968, may well have expressed new demands, ideas, and sensibilities, but they have analyzed them in old terms. The antinuclear movement, most of the regional struggles, and especially the women's movement, all have been strongly marked by leftist ideology, in the eyes of which they were new fronts in the war on capitalism, the axis of all conflicts. This mark ran so deep that when all the leftist actions ran out of steam—in France, this started in 1974-76—most observers declared dead the new social movements, which they identified with their leftist avatar. Let us recall, however, that the same misadventure plagued, in far more tragic fashion, the labor movement at its birth: the crises and the fall of the Second Republic, between 1848 and 1851, led people to think that syndicalism was dead. It was to reappear, under quite a different form, ten years later.

Isn't it normal for an emergent social actor to be subordinated to a better established force, such as a political party, an ideology, or even the social intervention of the State? Those who take snapshots of contemporary reality may conclude that they no longer see any social movements on their pictures, especially in France where social life has been leveled out by the effects of the economic crisis and the simultaneous decomposition of older ideologies, which survive only in official speeches. Strangely enough, it is in private life, in the least directly political expressions, such as songs, and in small intellectual groups, that one must seek the latent life of protests of a new sort.

Social movements are best delimited in these situations of conflictual pull between the past and the future; they serve as reminders to individual subjects that the latter are defined more by their creativity than by their creations, and more by their convictions than by the results they achieve. In their formative period, all the great social movements have drawn their capacity to resist and their hopes from the moral drive of their militants, which impelled them to refuse to submit to injustice on the one hand and to accept the proddings of wise counsel-givers that could lead them to compromise themselves, on the other. Behind the current return to the sphere of the private, the irresistible force of which is constantly being brought home to us, it may be possible to see a divorce from older ideologies and forms of action, at the same time as the malaise of a society without stakes, actors, or perspectives. And thus perhaps also to see, if not the presence of social movements, the pain of their absence and the desire for their return.

The Risk of Decadence

Having examined the chances of a new social movement emerging, one must wonder whether the current situation in Western European countries does not stand in the way of such an emergence. The theme, previously introduced, of the loss of hegemony by these countries may lead to a pessimist outlook. The study of dependent countries shows that their dualism, their disarticulation, is not limited to the economic sphere and touches the social movements themselves. There is affirmed in these countries a will to break with foreign domination, a will that leads to a guerrilla movement rather than a mass action; there is also affirmed an identity that takes the form of national or ethnic movements and leads to communitarian actions that may be autonomous or heteronomous. But never do the two components appear to coalesce and form a social movement. Is it possible that the Western countries, whose global influence is under increasing attack, are going through a similar split? On the one hand, we have communitarian movements, of which the ecological is the chief representative; they can close themselves off in a form of marginality, or, on the contrary, find themselves propelled to violent confrontation with the dominant order. On the other hand, there grow the denunciations of a manipulatory and alienating absolute order. A split occurs between theory and praxis, between thought and lived experience, which seems to permanently disorganize the social movements of North America and of Western Europe. The impact of such a split is limited, because the Western industrialized countries, even though they have lost their hegemony over the world, still remain privileged and dominant societies, and thus keep autonomous an inner dynamic vis-à-vis the action of a State engaged in a struggle for survival or for national liberation.

The struggles that animated the sixties and seventies cannot be identified either directly or completely with a new social movement. At best, they were its first manifestation, inseparable from a given historical and ideological conjuncture to the point that the conjoined crisis of expansion and of the New Left resulted in their decline. This historical conclusion does not invalidate the essence of the ideas introduced at the end of the sixties, however. An economic crisis may have followed an unprecedented period of growth, and the commingling of cultural innovations with social struggles may have been replaced with political crisis and social struggle behavior, but one may continue to think that a slow labor of formation of new social movements is taking place through successive historical sets of circumstances. Similar discontinuities occurred in the history of the labor movement in the nineteenth century. A first phase, in which social experimentation and utopia were dominant, was replaced by another, characterized by the intervention of political forces and even by the development of State Socialism. Only later was the labor movement able to affirm itself in its social reality.

Similarly today, after a phase in which we have seen struggles ebb and conflicts come apart, the maturing of a social movement is likely to profit from these beneficial factors in the near future. First, the conflicts between claim-making movements and the political system will become more virulent. The social and cultural reforms easily adopted during the past decades are likely to encounter ever stronger resistance from the silent majority. The United States, Great Britain, and later Germany are all examples of such conservative stiffening; it is difficult to imagine that, given their present situation, our societies will remain as permissive in the face of more pronounced claims and demands. Second, the maturing of the ruling class is taking place, especially its affirmation vis-à-vis the State. It is inevitable that in a phase of historical mutation, the role of the State should appear paramount; it happens at the beginning of all historical stages, and thus we see it at the onset of postindustrial society. But the more established the new type of society becomes, the more its internal relations, especially its defining class relations, are reinforced. Finally, intellectuals are returning to the analysis of the present instead of the reinterpretation of the past. All together, the formation of postindustrial society is sufficiently advanced for the perception and the study of new actors and their conflicts to contribute in turn to the development of the new societal type. It remains true that a large part of sociology is still beholden to the nineteenth-century idea that society is an organic or a mechanical system, with its own laws, and that the function of sociological analysis is to dispel the illusion of the actor. Such an approach excludes the existence of social movements a priori. It is increasingly important to defend another sociology, one that gives a central role to the idea of social movement and creates a new professional practice that attempts to apprehend actors in the awareness of their action, a sociology for which human beings make history knowing that they do so, while still being caught up in ideologies. An urgent need exists for developing new research approaches that look directly at social action itself, that study actors not only in their acts but also in the analyses they draw from these acts, and who attempt to bring out, beyond the response behavior imposed by a social order, the questioning behavior through which society produces itself conflictually. The formation of new social movements and the transformation of sociological analysis are inseparable.

Chapter 13
Social Movements, Revolution, and Democracy

The Idea of Progress

For a long time, the Western tradition did not separate social movements, democracy, and revolution. The notion of social movement, with the stress on "social," did not in fact exist: movements were defined as political; on the other hand, there seemed to be no difference between revolution and democracy. Revolution was the destruction of an Ancien Régime, of privileges, or of foreign domination; democracy was the political expression of the idea of progress and represented the triumph of reason. The American Revolution appeared by its very nature to be democratic in spite of its aristocratic features. Similarly, Bolívar thought of himself as the servant of universal values throughout his military campaigns and efforts to bring about a unified Latin America. During the French Revolution, however, the three ideas were considerably less integrated; 1789 remains a symbol of democracy; the Jacobin period is defined as revolutionary, and the Sans-Culottes, and even more so the urban laborers, were seen as social movements that could endanger the political revolution as much as come to its defense.

And thus there came to be a very long tradition which proclaimed that the three notions could not be separated because they were three aspects of the same general principle: progress. The assimilation of the three faces of progress did not prove to be lasting, however, not beyond the overturning of Anciens Régimes and of colonial domination. The idea of progress, adopted by very diverse social and political forces, was only reinterpreted in a variety of ways.

Capitalists were more interested in free enterprise than in public freedom, and in political liberty more than in the freedom of organization of social movements. Democracy was often reduced to a way of organizing a limited political system; social movements, for their part, were largely identified with the idea of revolution and with the social forces that had been excluded from the political system.

On a global scale, democracy was largely assimilated with dominant countries, whereas the rest of the world could only choose between a dependent participation, by nondemocratic means, in the democratic world, or violent struggles for its independence and development. Thus was the unity of the three notions quickly shattered and replaced by the opposition between two alliances: on one side, between social movements and revolution, on the other, between democracy and bourgeoisie. Once the old social order was broken, industrial society took its place, and its central conflicts quickly replaced the opposition between tradition and modernity.

From Progress to Industrial Conflict

The first, and the most important, aspect of the break with the idea of progress— whereby revolution, democracy, and social movements were confused—is the formation of the labor movement, at least if we give a precise definition to this notion which cannot be identified with all the aspects of syndicalism, or, even less, with labor relations. When syndicalism is primarily a form of organized action with the aim of achieving collective goals—a definition which corresponds to what has been called market or business syndicalism—it is neither democratic nor revolutionary, no more than the seller of any other commodity. But this type of syndicalism quickly lost importance as the labor market became more influenced by labor unions themselves as well as by oligopolistic strategies and State intervention. A second type of organized labor or syndical action gains importance then, intervening in the formulation of social and economic policies. In their analysis of the determinants of the frequency of strikes in France, Charles Tilly and Edward Shorter[1] give central importance to the changes that have come about in the political influence of labor visions. This is also the main conclusion of Colin Crouch and Alessandro Pizzorno[2] in their book on European organized labor. But how could one forget that labor laws and collective agreement were the result of powerful pressures, often of a revolutionary type, that originated outside the ranks of labor or outside the workers' movement. What matters most here is that this movement is no longer defined in terms of political participation or exclusion, but in terms of genuinely social conflict, in particular class conflict. The workers' movement is born from a direct conflict, on the factory floor, between employers and wage earners, and it is about working conditions. More precisely, this conflict appears directly tied to the destruction of the professional autonomy of workers as a result of rationalization, with salary schemes based on worker output as its most concrete expression.

The workers' movement reaches its highest development in mass production industries where directly productive skilled labor is replaced with semi-skilled or unskilled labor. Before this central phase in the evolution of work, workers were more autonomous and therefore defined and defended their interests in the labor market rather than inside the factory, either through negotiation or through violence. After this central phase, workers became incorporated in large organizations, and they no longer could oppose their skills and their autonomy to the organization of labor, being reduced to protest the hierarchized organization of the *Herrschaftsverband* (organization with a domination structure), as Max Weber called it.

It is tempting to hold that the workers' movement, defined as the agent of a structural conflict around the social use of technological resources, is revolutionary by nature because it is engaged in a central conflict with entrepreneurs and necessarily produces an ideology hostile to management and to capitalists. The first level (the economic level) of union action could thus be considered as autonomous, whereas its political level would be oriented by democratic values, and the direct class conflict would have an orientation governed by a revolutionary ideology. This conception has been broadly accepted, with most of the discussion concerned with the relative importance of each of these levels. But it must be rejected. Our analysis of the workers' movement insists on concrete labor relations, on the destruction of workers' control over their own production, and this is a properly social, and not a political, definition of the workers' movement. Its political orientation has less to do with its nature than with its environment. If its protests are readily accepted and processed by political institutions, it can take reformist or democratic forms; if, on the contrary, the political system is closed and authoritarian, social protest, having met with rejection, turns to challenge existing political institutions and becomes revolutionary. S. M. Lipset has given on several occasions, recently in his Presidential Address to the American Political Science Association, a very convincing demonstration of this type of correlation. The workers' movement even remains incapable of proposing a model of social and economic transformation. It is defined by a conflict and cannot go beyond the ideological expression of this conflict. It demands that factories should belong to workers or calls for self-management, but this does not constitute a political program. A class labor movement accepts its subordination to political action. Sometimes it submits to middle-class parties or even to conservative parties; in other cases, to populist parties; and finally in some cases, to workers' parties defined in Leninist fashion by the separation of political action from trade unionism. The workers' movement defends those who work and criticizes the irrationality it attributes to the industrial system, but, in order to get a rational use of technical resources, it must appeal to the State for the suppression or the limitation of the power of capitalists. In most cases, this intervention of the State is considered to be the direct effect of a mass mobilization, of an open conflict, or even of a general strike. The predominant role of political action has been affirmed by the revolutionary parties to whom economic action appeared unduly limited. The importance of the workers' movement for our analysis stems from the quite opposite fact that it proclaims the autonomy of social movements vis-à-vis all forms of political action, be they democratic or revolutionary. It is an independent and central social movement, but its field of action is limited to problems of production, so that it submits by itself to political action in order to change all of society.

The workers' movement represents a first, and still partial, attempt to ensure the autonomy of social movements. It separates the action of the workers against the management of enterprises from an anticapitalist political program. The first element is to be found in all countries at a certain stage in the evolution of industrial production; the second, on the other hand, is evident only in specific economic and political conditions. The first occurs equally in Polish and Brazilian enterprises today, just as it did in Detroit or Billancourt in the thirties; by contrast, every type of regime, capitalist or socialist, gives rise to particular political orientations that are then layered over the workers' movement in the strict sense, which is always and everywhere engaged in a conflict with the employers.

Whereas ancient social movements—from the peasant revolts of the seventeenth century to the rent strikes of the twentieth and including craftsmen movements in the fourteenth—were directly political and pressed the State to control the prices of staples and the minimum wage, the workers' movement is more social than political, even though it maintains ties with a political action to which it voluntarily subordinates itself. The autonomy of the labor movement as social movement is in direct proportion to class consciousness, whereas the revolutionary political orientation of the movement carries the day when economic and political conditions are more of a burden than bad working conditions.

The distance between workers' movement and democracy tends to grow larger in two different political situations. On the one hand, in some European countries, such as France, the political and ideological mobilization of a "progressive" middle class has been more important than the autonomous action of organized labor. In other countries, a fraction of the social movements has subordinated itself directly to political parties, while another, refusing to become implicated in the internal conflicts of the bourgeoisie, moved to antiparliamentarian positions, either on the Right or on the Left. Altogether different is the case of countries, such as Colombia and Mexico, in which the political system, endowed with a very strong capacity for integration and cooptation, is not organized along class divisions. These political systems were less involved in combating organized social movements than in keeping or pushing out of the political system large portions of the population by means of segregation or even violent expulsion. These political systems have worked with low levels of participation and have combined the political cooptation of the middle classes with State violence against the popular ones. In opposition to these two cases stand those countries in which the main political parties are organized along class lines and in which the political system has remained opened; the distance between democratic institutions and social movements has been more limited in such countries, as was true in England, and in Germany for long periods, and in Chile and Argentina.

To the separation between social movements and democratic institutions, a separation introduced by the labor movement itself in the nineteenth century, there has been added in the twentieth century a growing gap between social movements and revolution, and a clear separation between democracy and revolution at the world level. Revolutionary movements are less and less anticapitalist and increasingly anti-imperialist and anticolonialist. This has entailed the shift of revolutionary movements from industrial to nonindustrial countries, from the core to the periphery. Already noticeable after the Russian Revolution, this shift has had profound effects after World War II, as a result of the growing role of multinational corporations, the dramatic consequences of colonial wars in Asia and Africa, and the direct intervention of the Great Powers in the political life of numerous countries of the Third World. For their part, democratic regimes have succeeded in institutionalizing industrial conflicts, whereas in authoritarian regimes, claim-making movements have taken a revolutionary form. The ideas of democracy and of revolution thus find themselves corresponding to different areas of the world.

We see, then, through the nineteenth century and most of the twentieth, a progressive separation of the three notions which had initially been confused. They are no longer united in an evolutionist view of social life. Social movements, democracy, and revolution represent notions and regions that are not only different but often opposed to one another.

Left Intellectuals

Intellectuals have, by and large, participated in the decomposition of the progressive ideologies nourished by Enlightenment philosophy and the French and American revolutions. Some of these have identified with social movements, but in limited number, since these movements have frequently been anti-intellectual, especially when they espoused populist views. A larger number of intellectuals have turned into ideologues of democratic institutions and have identified them with general principles rather than with social forces or with specific social problems.

A smaller but more influential group of intellectuals has identified with revolution. Intellectuals are comfortable with a line of thinking that, having analyzed a system of domination, concludes that internal change is impossible and sees the necessity of opposing the natural laws of evolution to the resistance of acquired interests. The revolution must, or so they think, give power to science and knowledge, and to scholars and scientists against capitalists. The role of revolutionary intellectuals has been particularly important in the Communist movement, but one also finds them espousing Western anarchism and Russian nihilism.

What matters most, however, is that a significant portion of Western intellectuals, instead of identifying with social movements or democracy or even revolution, have sought to react against the progressive separation of these three themes and to reunite them, not in a practical or political manner, but in an ideological one. They have united these themes in a single sentence: social movements broaden and reinforce democratic institutions by their revolutionary action. The more democratic institutions, national liberation movements, and the syndicalist labor movement have drifted apart, the more intellectuals have proclaimed their unity. For more than a century, intellectuals have asserted with growing strength that class struggles, national liberation movements, and movements of cultural modernization were but different aspects of the same general conflict between the future and the past, between life and death. From the end of the nineteenth century until the mid-seventies, with more or less virulence depending on the country and the period, there has developed an ideology, or more exactly a myth, aiming at the reunification of forces that not only had separated but had begun to conflict with one another.

Some sought a reformist solution: the Fabians, S. and B. Webb in particular, introduced the idea of industrial democracy, which was used later, in an increasingly limited context, to account for the development of collective bargaining. Others, in different countries and at other times, looked for a more radical solution. This is where French intellectuals have played a central role, and so have some Third World intellectuals. From Anatole France to André Gide, from Andre Malraux to Jean-Paul Sartre, a long tradition of French intellectuals has viewed revolutionary regimes, socialist communist, and later the nationalist regimes of the Third World, as agents for widening and transformating a democracy that was too limited, too bourgeois. One could offer many interpretations of the phenomenon whereby so many intellectuals, spurred by the search for the unity of all the forces and forms of political and social transformation, came to support regimes far removed from old democratic principles.

But it is not the blindness of this number that matters; rather, it is the existence of an autonomous current of Left intellectuals, clearly distinct from revolutionary individuals, defenders of public liberties in their own countries and most often attacked as bourgeois intellectuals by authoritarian postrevolutionary regimes. These Left intellectuals have reacted against the growing separation of social movements, democracy, and revolution. In a first stage, they supported a new alliance between democracy and social movements, as did Rooseveltian liberal intellectuals in the United States and the French intellectuals who played a central role in the preparation of the Popular Front.

After the second World War, when the cold war and economic expansion reinforced right-wing governments in the West, a new generation of intellectuals, sensitive to the critique of Stalinism, sympathetic to the Polish October and to the Hungarian Revolution, as well as, later, to the Prague Spring, saw the Third World liberation movements as a new expression of popular and revolutionary forces with which liberal intellectuals in the West should ally in order to combat antidemocratic, imperialist, and racist forces in their own countries. Today, more and more critiques are addressed to these Left intellectuals who are accused of having been politically blind or even dishonest. Such a judgment is inadmissible for it amalgamates two completely opposite positions. On the one hand, some intellectuals have indeed identified with what they considered antibureaucratic and antiauthoritarian revolutionary movements. They opposed Stalinism in the name of Trotsky or of Marx and of a "genuine" socialist revolution. They were thus able to support the Chinese cultural revolution, in terms that were soon to be contradicted by the facts. In the West, these intellectuals created or recreated a doctrinaire "new old Left" which rapidly came to oppose quite often the new social or cultural movements. Nonviolent in France, these "fundamentalist" revolutionaries were more so in the United States and especially in Japan, Germany, and Italy.

On the other hand, the reference to Third World national and social movements was a way, for another group of Left intellectuals, to discover and support the new social movements that were emerging in their own countries. This tendency was particularly evident in the United States and in France at the end of the sixties. It has become predominant in nearly all countries during the seventies. This new Left has become more and more antirevolutionary and libertarian; it is opposed to the identification of social movements with State power. It has proclaimed the necessity of making political institutions more representative by opening them to new protests and new claims.

These three types of intellectuals, the Leninists, the revolutionary populists, and the libertarians, have sometimes united forces, especially during the French war in Algeria and the American war in Vietnam, and during the great French and American uprisings of 1968. But generally they have remained very distant from one another. In France, it was Jean-Paul Sartre, more than any other factor, who contributed to maintaining a certain unity among these divergent tendencies. He supported the May 1968 movement just as he had the anticolonial campaigns. He became the protector of the Proletarian Left, of Maoist orientation, without ceasing to define himself as a petit bourgeois, thereby signifying his will to defend Western democratic liberties. Upon his death, the crowd that accompanied his remains to the cemetery was conscious of the fact that, after him, it would no longer be possible to maintain a unity between actions and ideas ever more clearly contradictory.

Outside these three groups, some intellectuals had grown convinced some years earlier that it was impossible to integrate social and political forces so deeply divergent. Yet they tried to preserve the unity of social movements, democracy, and revolution, not in a positive and affirmative way, à la Sartre, but in a negative and purely critical manner, by proclaiming that all societies, liberal and postrevolutionary alike, were dominated by absolute power and that all aspects of social and cultural organization should be read as signs of the logic of this absolute domination, so that democracy is a lie, popular movements are impossible, and revolution is nothing but the destruction of popular movements. All these regimes, according to these intellectuals, call for the same revolt, the same rejection of a system of domination, alienation, and manipulation. This conception, which refuses any tie with organized social and political action, has become in some countries the specific ideology of disappointed revolutionary intellectuals. In France, this absolute determinism led to the conclusion that all organized collective actions are illusory, void of meaning, or even dangerous. In the aftermath of May 1968 this idea achieved predominant influence. Many intellectuals accepted the Althusserian conception according to which Marxism should be read as the scientific discovery of the internal mechanisms of a total domination that extends from the realm of production to all areas of social life.

During the same epoch, in Latin America, the same conception led revolutionary intellectuals to break with class action and mass movements and to put all their trust in guerrilla warfare to destroy systems of economic and political domination, the sole strength of which seemed to be the support of American imperialism. In Venezuela, Peru, and to some extent, with the Tupamaros, in Uruguay, these guerrillas acted in conformity with the ideas of a brilliant and courageous student of Althusser, Régis Debray.

But in Latin America, as in the industrial countries, these different orientations drifted apart. In Western Europe and in the United States, revolutionary intellectuals rapidly distanced themselves from the "radicals" linked to new cultural and social movements, whereas purely critical intellectuals, in the Marcuse tradition, theorized the impossibility of social movements and of revolutionary changes. In Latin America, after the failure of the guerrilla movement and the death of Che Guevara, some revolutionary groups, from Nicaragua to Peru, and, for a brief period, in Argentina, gave priority to armed struggle, whereas other groups, Christian in orientation or libero-radical, organized antiauthoritarian community movements at the grass-roots level.

These divisions mark the end of a movement whose intellectual and political influence was considerable, and at times even dominant, throughout a century. Its ideological failure, following the practical and political separation of the notions that had been united by Enlightenment philosophy and by the American and

French revolutions, marks the end of unitary attempts and the final separation of three terms that had been linked until then.

The End of Revolutions

The most immediate result of this division of Left intellectuals in the last quarter of the twentieth century is the decline of revolutionary ideologies. The era of revolutions is coming to an end. This may simply be because Anciens Régimes of all kinds have been destroyed almost everywhere and more people are suffering from the domination of modernizing authoritarian regimes than at the hands of conservative traditional elites. Already, at the beginning of the twentieth century, the Mexican Revolution was the reaction of the middle classes, the peasants, and the workers not against traditional landowners but against the rapid development of an agrarian and industrial capitalism dominated by foreign financial groups and by the actions of "cientificos" with their positivist and modernizing ideology. In Iran, in a different way, Khomeiny's shiite government put an end not to a traditional power but to a "white" revolution directed by the Pahlevi family and by foreign capital. In Poland, Solidarity, as a national and democratic social movement, fought the domination of a Communist party that defined itself as an agent of modernization and that destroyed what was, in some measure, an Ancien Régime.

In Western countries as well, the main protest movements are opposing presently an excess of transformation and voluntarist approaches to change rather than the absence of change. Progressive and revolutionary ideology counterposed open "society" to closed "community," the general rules of the State to the interests and particularist values of priests and landowners. The concentration of power is now so great that economic domination, political power, and cultural influence are often held in the same hands (in societies in which public investment plays a central role and in which the central control of information and communication is more important than the ownership of factories by monopolies). As a result, protest movements rise primarily against this concentration. Abandoning a long tradition, they reject the idea of revolution because the latter opens the door to the strengthening of State power. They are not counterrevolutionary but antirevolutionary in the sense that Spanish resistance to Napoleonic armies flying the French revolutionary flag was, or in the sense of the Czech workers who opposed an army that wrapped its tanks in the flag of the revolutionary workers' movement.

On the intellectual plane, the reaction against the transformation of social movements into authoritarian States has provoked a massive return of liberal ideology. France, where the influence of Left intellectuals had been the strongest, is the country with the most abrupt transformation in intellectual life. Raymond Aron lived long enough to acquire the certitude that his defense of democratic institutions and his attacks upon the "opium of intellectuals" had ultimately been accepted, on the Left as well as on the Right, and that the revolutionary ideology he had fought against was rejected by a vast majority, including Sartre's disciples.

A notable change is the importance and autonomy, newly acknowledged by social thought, of political categories and, above all, that of democracy. For a long time, democratic institutions had been criticized in the name of "real" democracy and of social justice; today, legal and institutional mechanisms of representation, and the free expression of interests, ideas, and protests, are finally being given the greatest importance. A growing number of Western intellectuals are studying the dangers in transforming popular movements into authoritarian regimes, whereas earlier their cares went to the social actors rejected outside these political systems.

It seems, then, that the idea of democracy has triumphed in the Western world, whereas the terms *democracy, social movement,* and *revolution* seem to have disappeared from the Communist world and to be in crisis in the Third World. After long years of dictatorship, Brazilians, Argentinians, Uruguayans, and Chileans all agree that the first of their goals is democracy and not revolution.

In parallel fashion, historians no longer give credence to the traditional idea that social movements are only preparatory stages to revolutions. French historians are challenging the notion that there was continuity in 1789-94,[3] and other historians are showing that syndicalism in Russia at the beginning of the twentieth century was something altogether different from a preparatory stage to the Bolshevik Revolution.[4]

Social Movements and Democracy

Let us begin by taking for granted the idea that the epoch of revolutions, inaugurated with the American and French revolutions and later prolonged by the Russian one, is coming to an end, and that there is a crisis of the scientistic and evolutionist thought upon which the action and the interpretation of revolutionary movements was constructed. Does this force us to conclude that the decline of the revolutionary model leads only to the triumph of an opposite political model, namely the democratic one? Or must we return to our main observation about the workers' movement and to the hypothesis that we are entering a period in which social movements become increasingly autonomous vis-à-vis their political expression? In such a case, the decline of the revolutionary should give as central a role to social movements as to institutional systems. We must recognize, however, that antirevolutionary attitudes are so strong in the West today that any reference to social movements is taken to be an indirect and confused way of saving some aspects of the declining revolutionary model. The very idea that political action "represents" social groups seems too beholden to the ideology of "real" democracy, as opposed to bourgeois democracy. Many analysts insist, on the contrary, on the autonomy of political institutions and on the balance of power even when they are critical of the negative effects of the excessive autonomy of the mechanisms whereby political leaders are selected.

In spite of the power of this intellectual trend, which stresses the central role of democracy and rejects the concept of social movement at the same time as that of revolution, let us try to uphold an opposite view, to observe the limits of a "purely" democratic conception, and to introduce the idea that social movements do occupy a central place and are the basic condition of democratic political life.

It is very risky today not to recognize the appearance of new social movements, just as it was for the parliamentary monarchs or the republic of the nineteenth century not to recognize the formation of the workers' movement. These new protest movements originate at an even greater remove from the political system than the workers' movement did, because they do not affect the division of labor or forms of economic organization, but, more deeply, cultural values. In their simplest form, they do not criticize the social use of progress, but progress itself. Sometimes they do so in a neotraditionalist way, but most often in such a way that the critique of industrial values reveals the reactions of cultural actors who are trying to keep, or to recover, control over their own behavior, in the same way that workers once did with respect to their working conditions. These movements are opposed to the large organizations that have the capacity to produce, distribute, and impose languages, information, and representations bearing upon nature, social order, individual and collective life. The very fact that these social movements are weak today and that their influence is more diffuse than organized shows their strong autonomy with respect to political institutions and in relation to the State. At a time when political life appears to be increasingly organized around the choice between economic policies, the new social movements deal with problems that are practically excluded from public life and that are taken to be private. They take positions on health, sexuality, information, and communication, and on the relation of life and death. Presently, all these problems appear to be farther removed from public life than labor problems were in industrial society.

The most general expression of these themes is to be found in the women's movement, which is also the most removed from the revolutionary model. Beyond the traditional theme of equality, beyond even the break with masculine domination in all of its forms and the appeal to an autonomous, specifically female culture, this movement has introduced new general protest aims. Traditionally, claims have been made in the defense of production against reproduction, and creation and change against social control and socialization, that is, they have in fact defended "active" roles, most often identified with men, against "reproductive" roles, identified with women. Now, rising against the growing concentration of power and the penetration of decision-making apparatuses into all aspects of social and cultural life, these protest movements take as their main objective not the conquest and the transformation of the State, but, on the contrary, the defense of the individual, of interpersonal relations, of small groupings, of minorities, against a central power and especially against the State. Women are transforming, or trying to transform, their status (which is inferior) and their culture (which is private) into an oppositional force against an instrumental and productivist culture.

The reference to minorities is already indicative of the fact that social movements are trying to limit their relations with the political system. To identify a social movement with the defense of majority rights is to identify social action and political struggle. The defense of minorities implies, on the contrary, that one is seeking to limit the extent of political intervention, to reject the idea that everything is political, to protect a nonpolitical though public area, something that represents a conception of public space—*Offentlichkeit*—quite different from that of previous societies.

But it is not enough to recognize the formation of these new social movements, which keep their autonomy from political parties and mechanisms. One must also recognize, and preeminently, that the force of democratic institutions rests upon their capacity to transform social conflicts into institutional rules, that is, upon their representationality. Democratic institutions have grown strong where the class conflicts of the industrial era were strong and recognized as central elements of a largely autonomous civil society. Where social classes had only limited autonomy, where the State and not the bourgeoisie was the chief agent of industrialization, where the working class gave way to an uprooted urban mass, democracy wound up weaker. It is overly pessimistic to say that democracy exists only where political power is limited. Such a situation could perfectly well lead to domination by local autocrats. In the same way, it is not enough to trust in favorable economic circumstances for the maintenance of democratic institutions, because the existence of a large surplus in no way ensures greater access of the majority to the instruments and the results of production.

Democracy must be identified with the notion of representativity, above all. This notion presupposes not only the existence of representative institutions but also that of representable social actors, that is, of actors who are defined, organized, and capable of action before they have any channel of political representation. If it is true that in some countries, especially those in Asia, democracy has been traditionally weakened by the existence of autocratic States, in other countries, chiefly in Latin America and in Africa, the main weakness of democracy in the twentieth century stems from the fact that social actors are not only controlled but created by the State, such as labor unions in Mexico and Brazil, and for a time in Argentina as well. The Western democracies are still strong because they have been able to transform the demands of the workers' movement into social laws and into rules governing industrial relations. But they are growing weaker presently because they are losing the capacity of transforming social movements into political forces. When political institutions cease to be representative and no longer provide channels and institutional solutions to social conflicts, they lose legitimacy. They take on the appearance of a set of pragmatic rules that, like those to be found in courtrooms, are used for the profit of the richest and the most informed. What makes the present situation serious is that it is more difficult now than it was earlier to build a representative democracy, precisely because the new social movements are less directly political than the old ones.

The transformations that have taken place in the relations between social movements, democracy, and revolution have led to the unification of these three forces within an evolutionist view of progress, which persisted until the occurrence of an increasingly complete separation of civil society, with its social movements, from the political system and the State. The workers' movement was the first to proclaim the autonomy and the central role of social movements, even though it kept itself subordinated to political action. The new social and cultural movements create a greater distance between social protest and political action. In many countries, the most urgent problems are those of economic development and of national independence. In these countries, social movements become ever more subordinate or are even destroyed, whereas protests, conflicts, and initiatives are organized directly around the conquest or the direction of the State. In other countries, such as those in Western Europe, social and cultural movements go as far as rejecting the State completely, even at the risk of playing into the hands of certain foreign States that they condemn more strongly than their own. It is true that such a separation between civil society and the State can reinforce the role of the political system and of the democratic institutions that serve as intermediaries between the social movements and the State. But it also runs the risk of isolating the political system from both the social movements and the State, and of downgrading it to the level of a simple political market that favors the most powerful pressure groups.

The most obvious consequence of this evolution is the growing gap between social movements and revolutionary action. The revolutionary image of social movements is in full decadence. At the same time, the gap between democracy and revolution has become so wide that the two notions appear contradictory to nearly everyone. Few people still believe that revolutionary action brings about democracy by itself, and regimes born of revolutions are heading into paths opposed to democracy.

The conception I have been developing is opposed to neoliberal thought, which finds itself logically reinforced by the decline of the revolutionary model.

One may even think that political debate will be more and more dominated by the opposition between those who help the new social movements find a mode of political expression and those who, on the contrary, accept the progressive incorporation of democratic institutions into the State apparatus in order to subordinate their representative functions to the defense of the national State, its international interests, and its economic policy.

Democratic institutions appear to have been reinforced in the Western world by the present crisis of the revolutionary model and by the weakness of social movements during a period of economic crisis and of lowered expectations. But these institutions become weaker when they do not recognize the priority and the autonomy of the new social movements, and the necessity of redefining themselves as representative while keeping their independence from State reason.

Postscript

1

Classical sociology, the "sociological tradition," was meant to be an analysis of modernity at the very moment the West was going through the consequences of the first industrial revolution. It was a stupendous idea which brought together hitherto separate fields of study. Evolutionism replaced the cyclical representation of civilizations and their natural history; rationality and efficacy appeared to define the meaning of modern societies better than the essence of their institutions; conflicts and ruptures were analyzed in terms internal to these modern societies rather than as effects of external threat or conquest.

And yet classical sociology was unable to achieve its own unity; it broke, permanently and insurmountably, into three currents of thought. The first, and closest to the earlier period, became concerned with the conditions of social order and integration; the second stressed relations of inequality and domination; the last tended to view modernity as the freedom of the market and the triumph of individualism. These three currents of thought were unified in the master concept of *society* only through the identification of modernity with the triumph of a ruling class as well as the reinforcement of the national State. This was a real intellectual power play that unified the problems relating to the functioning of industrial society with those of industrialization; yet it lost credibility as soon as capitalist industrial society ceased being the only model of industrialization. When "paths" to industrialization multiply, especially in the form of socialist or nationalist policies of industrial development, the identification of the State with social actors whose role is defined in a societal type, such as the bourgeoisie and the working class in Europe, is no longer possible and the concept of society collapses. The greatest classical sociologists attempted to overcome these internal contradictions of twentieth-century thought. Several sought to unite the idea of social system with that of modernization. Talcott Parsons, coming at the end of this classical period, tried to integrate Durkheim, Weber, and Tocqueville, at the cost of excluding the Marxist theme of structural conflicts. But the distance between these three representations resists all attempts at integration.

In the light of this state of affairs, I have sought here to reconstruct sociological knowledge, without occulting its internal debates and the plurality of its schools. In order to do so, I had to set aside two great notions upon which classical sociology was erected: society and evolution. Instead I situated at the core of analysis the cultural orientations common to actors who are in conflict over the management of these orientations, for the benefit of either an innovative ruling class or, on the contrary, those who are subordinated to its domination.

Classical sociology remained divided into a sociology of identity, that is, of the place occupied in the social system; a sociology of opposition, that is, of conflict; and a sociology of the totality of motion, that is, of modernity. I proposed the idea that the actors in conflict cannot be separated from the cultural stakes they have in common, and that the latter do not exist independently of the conflicts about their social use which oppose actors that we can name classes or social movements.

Those who tend to see in all aspects of social life the unrelenting presence of domination are reminded by this conception that dominated actors can also participate in a culture and therefore fight against the social domination to which this culture is subject. Those who see in social relations nothing but the diversified application of general norms and values are shown that between forms of organization and cultural orientations there stand distinguishable relations of domination in all collective practices. Those who continue to explain social facts by their position in a historical evolution find here the opposite idea: societies are less and less "in" history; they produce themselves their historical existence by their economic, political, and cultural capacity to act upon themselves and to produce their future and even their memory.

This break with classical sociology is possible only if we stop identifying actors with their works, subjects with history, if we abandon the epic vision, foundational of shifting political ideologies, in order to adopt a more romantic position, in order to recover actors in their confinement or in their solitude rather than in the triumph of their works. Hence the importance given to protest movements not only as specific objects of study but as the source of a more general origin of reflection, for it is in protest movements that innovation and revolt mix in order to disengage social actors from institutions as well as from ideologies, and to reveal both of these to be the indirect product of the cultural orientations and the social conflicts in which these actors are engaged.

2

Why is it difficult to carry out successfully the task of reconstructing sociological knowledge? Sociology is more directly affected than the other social sciences by immediate history, and we live practically—that is, politically and ideologically, rather than just intellectually—the crisis of the old representations of social life. Western societies' self-confidence, so evident in Talcott Parsons' great edifice as well as in the long tradition of positivism, was abruptly put to the test and challenged starting with the sixties. For critical sociologies to have any strong impact, they must counterpose a genuine historical model to the societies they challenge. Yet, at the present time, it is difficult to elicit enthusiasm or confidence in Moscow or Beijing, Algiers or Jerusalem, Havana or Belgrade. We have been disillusioned too many times to still believe in the promised land.

Finally, we have also come to doubt the idea of development, which would allow us to locate all countries along the path of a long march toward modernity and rationalization. Everywhere we see national specificities becoming more virulent; in many countries, community bonds are again becoming dominant in public life, even though Enlightenment philosophy thought it had swept them away from the modern world. The old images have crumbled into dust and we no longer have any thought of the social: its field is invaded by the action of States and their military rivalries on one side, and by personal and interpersonal problems on the other, as if there no longer obtained any autonomous public space.

This social void is the more noticeable as the political stage is generallly occupied by parties and coalitions that offer themselves as representations of groups, ideas, and projects that belong to an increasingly remote past. This state of affairs leads only to fatigue and skepticism: the discourse on social life no longer has analytical value, and, even in democratic countries, is perceived as a lifeless language of pieties and stereotypes.

Isn't it possible, though, that this somber picture lags behind the reality we are observing? Haven't our countries come to the realization that they were going through a crisis, and aren't they seeking to get rid of the old self-representations they had constructed? A society living in a mode of crisis has put sociology into crisis. In some countries, where the old models have retained more strength, the labor of renewing social thought is slow, as if public opinion preferred to flee the field of social thought rather than run the risk of coming up against words, ideologies, and programs that still have power even though almost no one believes in them. This seems to be the situation in France. In other countries, cultural transformations and the formation of a new cognitive model, of new ethical principles and new forms of investment and production, are more visible than the aging of political ideologies. Almost everywhere, though, the feeling of crisis is slowly making way for the idea of a mutation, a new stage in industrial or postindustrial development, and with it will come new social and political conflicts. This is why it is urgent to liberate the analysis of social life from lifeless ideas and words of only apparent clarity. Sociology, just like history, changes with social reality and slowly rids itself of the recourse to nature or to the essence of things, as our social life becomes more directly produced and transformed by our labor, our social conflicts, our cultural creations and our political debates.

3

We will never recover the historical certitudes of the founders of modern sociology, for whom history was a march toward individualism, rationality, or revolution. Today, the analysis of some collective behavior may lead us to the hypothesis that social movements are possible, but it is another thing to know under what conditions a real conflict becomes the bearer of a social movement, for sometimes a possible, and logical, movement fails to find historical expression. Three large questions of this type, on the boundaries of sociology and history, confront us today. First, are we still living in a civil society sufficiently independent from the State for cultural creations and social conflicts to occupy a central place, or have we, on the contrary, joined the bulk of the countries of the world whose societies are dominated by the voluntarist action of the State rather than by class conflicts? Second, is still possible to speak of social system, of a societal type defined by class relations and their cultural stakes, and hence by a central conflict, when change is accelerating and diversifying so much? Most observers do not think that a social movement as central as the workers' movement was to industrial society is likely to emerge in the future. For my part, I maintain that the reference to a central conflict is of the essence in any society endowed with historicity. The question is, however, whether we will go from defending this hypothesis to observing a central conflict in historical experience.

Third, aren't social movements torn between their reference to a nature capable of resisting technocratic manipulations and their will to utilize the most advanced techniques to transform the management of society? Social actors in the past had only a limited capacity because they were still in the midst of a world of reproduction rather than production. Today, the opposite situation obtains: are actors dismembered by accelerated change? This book does not provide answers to these questions; only a historical as well as sociological study of the forms of emergence and development of what I call programmed society can do so. But it has allowed us to formulate these questions. And they are as central today as was the following in the past century: how are stability and order created in a society constantly revolutionized by industrialization and its consequences?

This book has removed itself as far as it could from social history in order to give priority to the critical examination of the notions upon which sociological analysis rests. But its central objective is to make possible, and to pave the way for, the analysis of new social movements, of the new actors of our history. This is the reason for its title and the theme of all its chapters: to replace a sociology of society with a sociology of actors, and even of subjects, action systems, class relations, and conflicts, in short of social movements. More concretely, this volume aims at setting aside the old image of movements as historical agents of progress, of reason, and of science, and of a revolution that would suppress the irrationality of traditions and privileges in order to replace society into a natural order governed by functional and evolutionary laws. It wants to present social movements as collective actors engaged in a conflict for the social management of the main cultural resources. It shows that such a conflict can exist only in an open society, endowed with democratic institutions, and in the absence of any recourse to either the principle of a metasocial legitimation of the social order or the authority of an absolute State. The most general reflection most naturally comes upon the problems that affect us the most, for is there a more basic change than the one that separates, under our very eyes, the idea of social movement from that of revolution, henceforth compromised by the degeneration of postrevolutionary regimes, in order to link it with that of democracy, of political freedom, long the object of contempt for being "bourgeois," but without which social actors can neither fight nor negotiate? To assert this is not to submit sociological analysis to political goals; on the contrary, we shed the light of sociological analysis upon the political field when we place at the center of our present reflection two problems: how is the autonomy of civil society and of its actors to be preserved and developed in relation to a State that manages more and more directly economic, social, and cultural life? and how is the alliance between social movements and political democracy to be built?

These questions cannot be answered by only defining the requirements and the orientations of the new social movements. It is as important, and even more urgent today, to free the subject from the technical illusions, the bureaucracies, the political games, and the absolute powers that stifle it and seek to destroy it.

For a long time, the appeal to the subject, to human beings' capacity to make their own history, took the form of historical projects: to destroy privileges, to change institutions, to take power. These appeals were supposed to set in motion masses excluded from history. Today, the world no longer suffers from being too empty or too silent; it is filled with sound and fury. This is not the time for appeals to collective action; the moment has come to recall the subject. Not only is historicity an investment in cultural models; it is just as much a removal from the norms and practices of social consumption. Later, the hopes and the construction of new initiatives will return; today, the great battles are defensive and liberating: we must free ourselves from the great principles that have turned into small-minded strategies, from powers that have become aggressive or simply all-pervading.

The passage from one type of society to another can be accomplished at the point of a sword or, on the contrary, through internal transformations happening at the base of social life. The West is defined by the fact that it has created the most endogenous type of change, even if the latter was always supplemented by hegemony over the rest of the world. In the Western model of development, culture is always first to change: new knowledge and new techniques emerge, and they are associated with changes in mores and in forces of production. Then, new social actors come into being with their mode of action; later yet, the political system is reorganized and new forms of organization are put into place; finally, ideologies solidify, which correspond to the interests of the newly constituted actors.

At present our culture has been largely transformed: science and technology, on one side, ethics, on the other, and finally the forms of production are undergoing mutations. We think, we behave, and we work under the guidance of models that are no longer those of industrial society, but our forms of action and our political ideologies are still those of the past, even though they have entered into a process of irreversible decomposition. Between a transformed culture and forms of social organization and thought that remain attached to the past, it is difficult for social actors to come into being. Neither rulers nor ruled have a clear consciousness of themselves and of the conflicts that oppose them. This is the stage of the mutation at which our reflection is located: that of the passage from a historicity, from cultural models, already transformed to the yet uncertain formation of new actors. This passage is not mechanical; it occurs only if the cultural stakes stop having the appearance of a situation, if actors constitute themselves by orienting themselves toward them and discovering, by the same token, the domination relations in which they are placed.

What is the subject if not the social actor in relation to the cultural models, the historicity of the societal type in which she or he is placed? Only by means of the relation to the subject can we go today from a transformed culture to the formation of actors capable of animating it with their beliefs and their conflicts. We no longer hear appeals for the transformation of society or of the State; we distrust all mobilizations and all ideologies, but we do feel the need to inhabit the world we have already reconstructed instead of camping on its outskirts, in the ruins of our history.

Even in the most privileged situations, the passage from one societal type to another does not happen without discontinuity, and it is at this moment of rupture that it is most necessary to pay heed to the appeal to the subject, and to think of social situation not as that which rules action and consciousness, but as that which results from cultural innovations and social conflicts. Even before actors can recognize themselves as the creators of their own history, there must come what I have called the romantic moment, when subjects come to an awareness not of their works but of the distance that separates them from a hostile or meaningless order of things, in their desire for freedom and creation. Tomorrow new social movements and political negotiations are likely to be built up; today does not belong only to the decomposition of the past and to a general feeling of crisis, but to the recall of the subject, to the casting of doubt on all forms of social organization, and to the demand for creative freedom. This book wants to be located at this precise moment. It does not merely reflect upon the return of the actor; it prepares it.

Notes

Notes

Foreword

1. Talcott Parsons, *Social Systems* (Glencoe, Ill.: Free Press, 1964) and, with Edward Shils et al., *Toward a General Theory of Action* (New York: Harper and Row, 1951) and *Essays in Sociological Theory* (Glencoe, Ill.: Free Press, 1964).

2. The works of Claude Lévi-Strauss and Louis Althusser are particularly relevant here. See especially Claude Lévi-Strauss, *Savage Mind* (Chicago: University of Chicago Press, 1968) for general statements of his position. Louis Althusser's *For Marx* (New York: Schocken Books, 1979) and, with Etienne Balibar, *Reading Capital* (New York: Schocken Books, 1979) signal the Marxist turn toward epistemological issues, but also the critique of humanism which in his discourse is identified with historical agency.

3. The crucial text is Robert K. Merton, *Social Theory and Social Structure* (Glencoe, Ill.: Free Press, 1968).

4. Alvin W. Gouldner, *The Coming Crisis in Western Sociology* (New York: Basic Books, 1980).

5. See Robert K. Merton, *On Theoretical Sociology: Five Essays, Old and New* (Glencoe, Ill.: Free Press, 1967).

6. Erving Goffman, *Presentation of Self in Everyday Life* (New York: Doubleday, 1959), *Asylums: Essays on the Social Situation of Mental Patients and Other Inmates* (New York: Doubleday, 1961), and *Frame Analysis: An Essay on the Organization of Experience* (Cambridge, Mass.: Harvard University Press, 1974); Harold Garfinkel, *Studies in Ethnomethodology* (Oxford: Basil Blackwell, 1985); Aaron V. Cicourel, *Method and Measurement in Sociology* (Glencoe, Ill.: Free Press, 1964).

7. For the most general treatment of Alain Touraine's theoretical position, see *The Self-Production of Society*, trans. Derek Coltman (Chicago: University of Chicago Press, 1977).

8. C. Wright Mills, *Power Elite* (New York: Oxford University Press, 1956).

9. Paul A. Baran and Paul M. Sweezy, *Monopoly Capital: An Essay on the American Economic and Social Order* (New York: Monthly Review Press, 1968).

10. Alain Touraine, *The May Movement: Revolt and Reform*, trans. Leonard F. X. Mayhew (New York: Random House, 1971).

11. Lewis S. Feuer, *Einstein and the Generations of Science* (New Brunswick, N. J.: Transaction Books, 1982); Karl Mannheim, "The Problem of Generations," in *Essays on Sociology and Social Psychology* (Mannheim's superb essay should not be confused with Feuer's psychologizing social movements).

12. Alain Touraine, *Post-Industrial Society*, trans Leonard F. X. Mayhew (New York: Random House, 1971).

13. Henri Lefebvre, *Explosion: Marxism and the French Revolution* (New York: Monthly Review Press, 1969); Fredy Perlman, *Student and Worker Committees* (Detroit: Black and Red, 1968). See also Richard Baum, *Prelude to Revolution: Mao, the Party & the Peasant Question* (New York: Columbia University Press, 1975), for a classical Marxist view of the May events that ascribes the movement's defeat to its failure to forge a political alliance with the working class, especially its refusal to form a new revolutionary Socialist party.

14. Alvin W. Gouldner, *The New Class and the Future of Intellectuals* (New York: Seabury Press, 1981).

15. Karl R. Popper, *Logic of Scientific Discovery* (New York: Science Editions, 1961).

16. Jean-Paul Sartre, *Critique of Dialectical Reason* (New York: Schocken Books, 1983). Touraine has a fully developed conception of social structure which simply falls outside Sartre's social theory. For Sartre, "society" is constituted by actions that become sediments. Touraine's retention of the notions of accumulation and class relations, as well as his broader idea of the cultural model, saves his theory from the reductionism inherent in all theories of society as action.

17. Alain Touraine et al., *Solidarity: The Analysis of a Social Movement: Poland, 1980-1981*, trans. David Denby (Cambridge: Cambridge University Press, 1983), p. 5.

18. The originality of this critique is quite striking. That it embraces one of the central figures of the Frankfurt School, Marcuse, for whom agency was the major question posed by the emergence of advanced capitalist and industrial rationality, shows clearly how structuralist ideas permeate social theory. Touraine's argument points to the "death of the actor" as the core feature of structuralism in relation to the question of historicity.

Introduction

1. See in particular Alain Touraine, *Production de la Société* (Paris: Seuil, 1973).

Chapter 1. From Society to Social Action

1. Richard Sennett, *The Fall of Public Man* (New York: Knopf, 1974).
2. Christopher Lasch, *The Culture of Narcissism* (New York: Norton, 1978).

Chapter 2. The Mutation of Sociology

1. In particular, Erving Goffman, *The Presentation of Self in Everyday Life* (New York: Doubleday, 1959).

Chapter 3. The Crisis of Modernity

1. Barrington Moore Jr., *Social Origins of Dictatorship and Democracy* (Boston: Beacon Press,1966). Reinhard Bendix, *Nation Building and Citizenship* (New York: Wiley, 1975). Immanuel Wallerstein, *The Capitalist World Economy* (Cambridge: Cambridge University Press, 1979).

Chapter 4. Does Social Life Have a Center?

1. J. G. March and H. A. Simon, *Organizations* (New York: Wiley, 1958). M.Crozier and E. Friedberg, *L'Acteur et le système* (Paris: Seuil, 1977).

2. Clark Kerr et al., *Industrialism and Industrial Man* (Cambridge, Mass.: Harvard University Press, 1960). John T. Dunlop, *Industrial Relations Systems* (New York: Holt, 1958). A. Flanders and H. A. Clegg, ed., *The System of Industrial Relations in Great Britain* (Oxford: Blackwell, 1960).

3. Albert Hirschman, *The Strategy of Economic Development* (New Haven, Conn.: Yale University Press, 1958).

Chapter 6. Social Movements:
Particular Object or Central Problem of Sociological Analysis?

1. Neil Smelser, *Theory of Collective Behavior* (New York: Free Press,1962).

2. See Roger Girod, *Politiques de l'éducation* (Paris: P.U.F., 1981).

3. This theme was developed by Jean Foucambert in *Évolution comparative de quatre types d'organisation à l'école élémentaire* (Paris: I.N.R.D.P., 1977-79).

4. William Foote Whyte, *Street Corner Society* (Chicago: University of Chicago Press, 1965).

Chapter 9. The Method of Action Sociology:
Sociological Intervention

1. F. J. Roethlisberger and W. J. Dickson, *Management and the Workers* (Cambridge, Mass.: Harvard University Press, 1939).

2. S. Moscovici, *Psychologie des minorités actives* (Paris: P.U.F., 1979).

3. W. Doisé, *L'Explication en psychologie sociale* (Paris: P.U.F., 1983).

Chapter 10. The Birth of Programmed Society

1. Carl Polanyi, *The Great Transformation* (New York: Farrar, 1944).

2. Karl Deutsch, *Nationalism and Social Communication* (Cambridge, Mass.: M.I.T. Press, 1962).

3. Gino Germani, *Política y sociedad en una época de transición* (Buenos Aires: Editorial Sur, 1971).

4. Marshall Sahlins, *Stone Age Economics* (New York: Aldine Press, 1972).

5. Pierre Clastres, *La Société contre l'État* (Paris: Éd. de Minuit, 1974).

Chapter 11. The New Social Conflicts

1. See John Harry Goldthorpe, *The Affluent Worker*, 3 vols. (Cambridge: Cambridge University Press, 1968-69).

Chapter 13. Social Movements, Revolution, and Democracy

1. Charles Tilly and Edward Shorter, *Strikes in France, 1830-1968* (Cambridge: Cambridge University Press, 1974).

2. Colin Crouch and Alessandro Pizzorno, eds., *The Resurgence of Class Conflict in Western Europe since 1968* (London: Macmillan, 1978).

3. François Furet, *Penser la Révolution française* (Paris: Gallimard, 1978).

4. Victoria Bonnell, *Roots of Rebellion* (Berkeley and Los Angeles: University of California Press, 1983).

Index

Index

Alain Touraine is a professor at L'École des Lettres et des Science Humaines at Paris-Nanterre. Several of his books have been translated into English, including *Solidarity: The Analysis of a Social Movement: Poland 1980-1981*.

Myrna Godzich was co-translator of Malek Alloula's *Colonial Harem* (Minnesota, 1986).

Stanley Aronowitz is a professor at the City University of New York and author, with Henry Giroux, of *Education Under Siege*.